STATISTICAL GRAPHICS FOR UNIVARIATE AND BIVARIATE DATA

WILLIAM G. JACOBY
University of South Carolina

SAGE PUBLICATIONS
International Educational and Professional Publisher
Thousand Oaks   London   New Delhi

For information address:

 SAGE Publications, Inc.
2455 Teller Road
Thousand Oaks, California 91320
E-mail: order@sagepub.com

SAGE Publications Ltd.
6 Bonhill Street
London EC2A 4PU
United Kingdom

SAGE Publications India Pvt. Ltd.
M-32 Market
Greater Kailash I
New Delhi 110 048 India

Printed in the United States of America

Library of Congress Cataloging-in-Publication Data

Jacoby, William G.
    Statistical graphics for univariate and bivariate data /
author, William G. Jacoby.
        p. cm.—(Quantitative applications in the social sciences; vol. 117).
    Includes bibliographical references (p.).
    ISBN 0-7619-0083-7 (pbk.)
        1. Statistics—Graphic methods. I. Title. II. Series: Sage university papers series.
    Quantitative applications in the social sciences; no. 117.
    QA276.3.J33   1997   96-45892
    001.4'226—dc21   CIP

97 98 99 00 01 02 03 10 9 8 7 6 5 4 3 2 1

Acquiring Editor:	C. Deborah Laughton
Editorial Assistant:	Eileen Carr
Production Editor:	Sherrise M. Purdum
Production Assistant:	Denise Santoyo
Copy Editor:	D. J. Peck
Typesetter/Designer:	Yang-hee Syn Maresca

CONTENTS

SERIES EDITOR'S INTRODUCTION

In the presentation of empirical results, we make an argument. Explication of the study design, sample, measures, and coding procedures informs readers about the quality of our work. The statistical findings we report, from the operations on the data gathered, provide the systematic evidence for our conclusions. But how persuasive are those conclusions? To a great extent, it depends upon how well we make the data speak. The standard analytic line involves a marshalling of summary statistics: means and standard deviations, measures of association; multiple regression coefficients. Such summaries are efficacious, saying in a single number something of general importance about the diverse data under examination. But they do not go far enough. As this splendid paper by Professor Jacoby makes abundantly clear, you need also to show the data.

Take an example using the standard deviation. Suppose Professor Mary Green, on the Ed Psych faculty, is investigating the distribution of the grade point among the 3,000 sophomores at her university. From the sample data (N = 300), she calculates mean G.P.A. = 2.8, standard deviation = .40. As a preliminary assessment, she guesses that about 95 percent of the sophomore population has a G.P.A of 2.8, plus or minus .78 [i.e., +/- 1.96 (.40) = .78]. She knows that inference depends on the assumption that grade-point is normally distributed in the population. Is it? To answer that question, she applies two tests to the sample data: a mean-median-mode comparison, and the skewness statistic. She finds mean = 2.8, median = 2.8, and mode = 2.5; skewness = .30. Dr. Green decides that the normality assumption is met, at least approximately. Perhaps, but after reading Jacoby, I would urge her to go beyond these summary numbers, and look at the data. Namely, examine the histograms, quantile plots, and box plots. There may be modalities, outliers, humps, skews or other abberations of great interest to be seen there.

The data picture helps complete, or even tells, the story. But sometimes analysts do not show the data because the data appear to confuse, rather than enlighten. When that happens, it may simply be that the manner of visualization was faulty. The scatterplot is the classic visual in quantitative

v

social science. It has the formidable power to convey, immediately and intuitively, how two variables are related. However, this power disappears if the figure is poorly done. Professor Jacoby gives careful guidelines here for filling in the scale retangle: use readable symbols, avoid overplotting, make tick marks outward, do not make too many tick marks, transform the values when necessary. While these rules seem eminently sensible, they are often violated in the literature. Overplotting, which occurs when too many points are at virtually the same location, can be overcome by the technique of jittering, which introduces just enough random variation into the observations to separate the points for visual inspection. Even assuming that the scatterplot properly displays the data, it can be difficult to discern the functional form of the relationship, if it is not linear. A valuable procedure here is scatterplot smoothing, in particular the use of the loess smoother. Loess, which stands for locally weighted regression, forms a smooth line through the point cloud by estimating a series of moving, subset, regressions. The resulting curve represents the unique function form of that relationship.

In an earlier paper, I advocated what I called "eyeballing." For the first look at interrupted time series scatterplots, as a way of making an initial assessment of the presence of policy intervention effects (Lewis-Beck, 1986). The notion was that an intervention might not show up in the estimated interrupted time series equation, but be revealed by the naked eye. Of course, that revelation would suggest that the equation was improperly specified. Thus, inspection of the plot could improve the model. Professor Jacoby renders a more general principle: visualize the data, in order to find out what's really going on.

—*Michael S. Lewis-Beck*
Series Editor

♦

Special thanks go to Saundra K. Schneider. This monograph could not have been completed without her advice, assistance, encouragement, and support. Several other people read earlier drafts of the manuscript and provided excellent feedback. In particular, I would like to thank Ulf Bockenholt, William Cleveland, Jeff Coon, John Fox, Charles Franklin, Paul Lewicki, Michael Lewis-Beck, Stefanie Lindquist, Herbert Weisberg, and Forrest Young for their great help during the entire course of this project. The monograph has benefited immeasurably from their contributions.

STATISTICAL GRAPHICS FOR UNIVARIATE AND BIVARIATE DATA

WILLIAM G. JACOBY
University of South Carolina

1. INTRODUCTION

The purpose of statistical graphics is to provide visual representations of quantitative information. Graphs always have been an important part of the statistical sciences (e.g., Beniger & Robyn, 1978). But in the past they were used primarily for pedagogical purposes and for the presentation of final analytic results. More recently, graphical displays have been incorporated directly into the data analysis. As a methodological tool, statistical graphics comprise a set of strategies and techniques that provide the researcher with important insights about the data under examination and help guide the subsequent steps of the research process.

The evolution of statistical graphics in this direction probably has been facilitated by three related sets of developments. First, there have been major advances in graphical methodologies (e.g., Chambers, Cleveland, Kleiner, & Tukey, 1983; Cleveland & McGill, 1988). These include completely new tools for providing immediate graphical representations of complex data sets (Young, Faldowski, & Harris, 1990; Young, Faldowski, & McFarlane, 1993) along with closer attention to the graphical aspects of other well-known statistical procedures (Cook & Weisberg, 1994). Second, there has been a great deal of recent research conducted on the psychology of graphical perception (e.g., Cleveland, 1994; Cleveland & McGill, 1984a; Kosslyn, 1985). This line of work has led to important insights about the most effective strategies for presenting quantitative information in visual form. Third, the rapid evolution and widespread availability of powerful computing equipment has been crucial for graphical applications. The fast, high-resolution graphical capabilities of desktop computers, along with the development and dissemination of appropriate software (e.g., Becker, Chambers, & Wilks, 1988; Stine & Fox, 1996; Tierney, 1990;

Young, 1996), help create the type of working environment that is absolutely necessary for the effective deployment of statistical graphics during the data analysis process. Taken together, these three general developments have placed graphical methods alongside more traditional numeric approaches in the statistical sciences.

What This Monograph Is (and is not) About

The purpose of this monograph is to present the major techniques that fall under the general heading of statistical graphics. The primary focus of the discussion is on *analytic* graphics. In other words, I concentrate on graphical techniques that the researcher would employ as an integral part of the data analysis process. There is little explicit coverage of so-called *presentational* graphics or the kinds of displays that are intended primarily for communicating completed analyses to a lay audience.

The differences between analytic and presentational graphics are a bit subtle but nevertheless quite important. These two kinds of displays are used for very different purposes. Analytic graphics help show the researcher what is salient and interesting in the data under consideration. As John Tukey (1977), one of the pioneers in this field, puts it, a visual representation of data "forces us to notice what we never expected to see" (p. vi). On the other hand, presentational graphics assume that the important features of the data are already known to the researcher, and they create visual representations of these features for other audiences. Kosslyn (1994) explains that "a good graph forces readers to see the information the designer wanted to convey" (p. 271). To reiterate, this work focuses almost entirely on graphical techniques that are employed in the course of a data analysis. Nevertheless, it is my experience that carefully constructed analytic graphs also are quite effective for presentational purposes.

The Objectives of Graphical Methods

Graphical statistical methods tend to be employed to achieve four broad and mutually supportive objectives. First, they are useful for exploring the contents of a data set. Visual displays are particularly well suited for an investigator's initial cut at the data because they avoid many of the subtle assumptions that underlie numerical summary values. Statistical graphics can be used to address questions about the variables in an analysis (e.g., what are the distributional shapes, ranges, typical values, or unusual observations?). And because well-constructed graphs can incorporate a very large amount of quantitative information in a very efficient manner, the researcher can use them to observe and comprehend a larger segment of his or her data in a single view than is possible with traditional statistical summaries. To put it simply, statistical graphics facilitate our understanding of the information that is contained within raw data.

Second, statistical graphics are used to find structure in data. They differ from most traditional methods in that they try not to make stringent assumptions about the nature of that structure. For example, a typical regression analysis proceeds by trying to express a dependent variable as a linear combination of a set of independent variables. But this is in itself a very rigid statement about the ways in which the variables are related to each other. As an alternative approach, a plot of the data could be examined directly to see whether patterned regularities appear in the visual display. If so, then they should supply vital information about the appropriate kind of mathematical function to express the relationships within the data. The connections among the variables may well be linear, in which case traditional regression methods are perfectly appropriate. On the other hand, if there is a nonlinear relationship, then the visual approach saves the investigator the trouble of fitting a model that is incorrect, working through the diagnostics to discover the error, and then taking corrective action. Thus the graphical approach may well provide a more direct route to the ultimate goal of theory construction. As Tukey (1977) says, these kinds of methods are used to "look at the data and see what it seems to say" (p. v).

Third, graphical methods can be used for checking assumptions in statistical models. Empirical analyses seldom stop at description of a set of observations. Instead, the goal usually is to generalize from the observed data to some broader unobserved population. But the ability to do so requires stringent assumptions about the nature of the processes that are generating the data in the first place. If these assumptions are not met, then any conclusions drawn from the analysis are compromised. Although all good statistical procedures contain diagnostic tests for examining their own assumptions, the degree to which these are employed in practice probably is woefully small. Direct visual representations of a statistical model and, perhaps more important, the residuals from the model greatly facilitate the examination of assumptions. In so doing, they make it easier to identify problematic aspects of the model's fit to the data. Furthermore, some "active" graphical approaches allow the researcher to interact directly with model parameters and data points; this enables one to examine various "what if?" scenarios before deciding on a final functional representation of the data. In sum, visual methods should encourage the researcher to make much more effective use of the statistical modeling tools that already are available than typically has been the case in the past.

Finally, statistical graphics are very useful for communicating the results of an analysis. This may seem to be stating the obvious, but it still is important. The human visual processing system provides an incredibly effective means for understanding complex information. The implications of numerical summaries often are more easily comprehended when shown as a picture. Despite this fact, graphical displays of data and statistical models are surprisingly rare in scientific publications, and this is particularly the case in the social sciences.

The Advantages of Graphical Approaches to Data Analysis

The advantages to be gained through the use of statistical graphics are perhaps best illustrated by a simple example. Table 1.1 displays hypothetical values for 20 observations on each of four variables. This certainly is not a large data set, yet visual inspection of the numeric values probably does not lead to any useful insights. The obvious remedy is to employ some data reduction strategy to decrease the overall amount of information that immediately confronts the observer. For example, summary statistics could be calculated for each of the variables. The latter transcend the excess detail contained in the separate observations and focus directly on the salient characteristics of the variables' distributions (the location of the distribution centers, the dispersion in the variable values, etc.). Accordingly, the sample means and standard deviations are shown at the bottoms of the columns in Table 1.1.

The summary statistic values are identical across the columns. The fact that all four variables have the same means and standard deviations, perhaps combined with the informal observation that most of the values in the data matrix fall within a common interval ranging from about 20 to 40, could easily lead an unwary observer to the conclusion that these variables have similar, if not identical, distributions. But this definitely is *not* the case, a fact that is revealed immediately by the graphical evidence presented in Figure 1.1. The figure graphs the data from Table 1.1, using unidimensional scatterplots for each of the four hypothetical variables. This kind of graphical display is discussed more fully in Chapter 2. For now, it is only necessary to mention that each plotting symbol represents a separate observation; therefore, the concentration of data points at any

TABLE 1.1
Hypothetical Data Matrix Containing 4 Variables and 20 Observations

Observation Number	X_1	X_2	X_3	X_4
1	32.3	33.2	24.7	29.7
2	28.0	34.2	29.4	30.2
3	31.4	27.0	28.5	28.7
4	29.5	33.0	25.6	27.3
5	40.0	35.8	27.6	31.3
6	20.0	34.6	32.0	29.5
7	26.0	24.2	28.2	26.3
8	28.6	34.9	40.9	29.9
9	27.7	25.1	37.5	29.8
10	27.0	37.3	26.3	30.1
11	17.5	22.7	33.9	37.9
12	31.0	25.4	36.7	27.6
13	32.0	25.8	25.2	30.3
14	30.5	38.2	23.8	22.1
15	34.0	26.5	26.1	28.1
16	42.5	38.4	28.2	26.5
17	35.0	26.8	31.8	30.5
18	29.0	21.6	39.7	27.4
19	25.0	33.5	19.1	51.0
20	33.0	21.8	34.8	25.8
Mean	30.0	30.0	30.0	30.0
Standard deviation	5.8	5.8	5.8	5.8

numerical value within a variable's range can be approximately equated to the ink density (i.e., the overlap of the plotting symbols) at that position along the horizontal axis (which provides a common numerical scale for all four variables). These unidimensional scatterplots show clearly that the variable distributions differ from each other in important and easily recognizable ways. For anyone confronted with the information in this graphical form, there is no question that the variables have divergent distributions. Instead, attention would center on the more interesting question of why the four sets of values show such systematic differences from each other.

This brief example illustrates very nicely the advantages of graphical approaches to data analysis.[1] First, graphs provide useful summaries for large, complicated data sets. Humans simply are incapable of processing information about lengthy numerical arrays. Graphs provide an effective means of downplaying the details of the data (i.e., the specific values) and

6

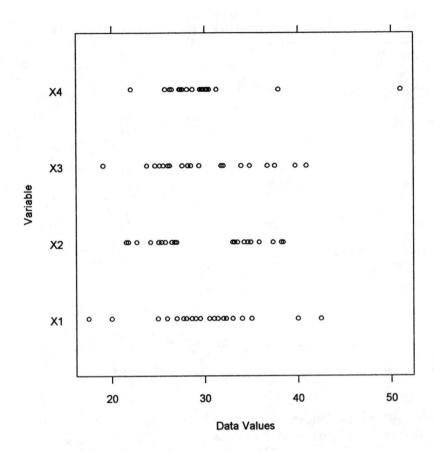

Figure 1.1. Univariate Scatterplots Comparing Data Distributions of Four Hypothetical Variables
SOURCE: Data from Table 1.1.

emphasizing the important features (the distributional shape, location, presence of unusual observations, etc.). Even a cursory glance at Figure 1.1 reveals that X_1 has a unimodal, symmetric distribution, whereas the distribution for X_2 is symmetric but bimodal. At the same time, X_3's distribution is skewed positive, whereas X_4's distribution is compressed to the left (i.e., centered around somewhat lower values than the others) but offset by a single outlying observation with an extremely large value.

Of course, summarization traditionally has been accomplished through the use of descriptive statistics. But this leads to the second advantage of the graphical approach: All numerical summaries of data are based on assumptions about the nature of those data. If these assumptions are met, then descriptive statistics provide an accurate representation of the data's features. But to the extent the assumptions are not met, descriptive statistics can be inaccurate and misleading. Once again, consider Figure 1.1. The sample mean and standard deviation are accurate summaries of the distribution for X_1, but they seriously misrepresent the other four variables. Graphical presentations are not nearly as reliant on such underlying assumptions, and so they can be used to summarize the data without the attendant dangers of misrepresentation.

A third advantage is that graphical analysis facilitates greater interaction between the researcher and the data. Effective visual presentations highlight interesting and unusual aspects of the quantitative information under investigation. This encourages the researcher to pursue these features to identify their sources and implications for understanding the processes that are generating the data in the first place. For example, the bimodal nature of X_2's distribution immediately raises questions about the existence of important subgroups within the data set. Similarly, the outlier in the X_4 distribution is hard to miss; therefore, it is easy to identify the specific observation corresponding to this point and examine it more closely.

The preceding discussion raises some fundamental questions. Is it always advantageous to employ a graphical display? Are there any situations in which tabular displays are better than graphs? Although there are no definite, clear-cut answers to these questions, a few general guidelines can be stated to help the researcher determine the most effective strategies for presenting quantitative information (e.g., Ehrenberg, 1975; Fox, 1992; Kosslyn, 1994; Tufte, 1983, 1990).

Tables are useful for conveying specific numeric values, particularly when the number of data points is not too large (say, seven or fewer). In fact, graphs can be somewhat detrimental in such situations because it often is difficult to recover the numeric values from the visual display. In contrast, graphs usually are superior for revealing patterns, trends, and relative quantities within data sets regardless of their size. But the latter is precisely the kind of information that one usually wants to obtain from a data analysis; numbers rarely are presented as an end in themselves. Therefore, graphs should be very helpful for a wide variety of purposes in empirical research.

Graphical Perception

When a researcher employs the tools of statistical graphics to achieve some analytic objective, there are two interacting components involved in the process. On the one hand, there is the graph itself, which *encodes* numeric information in pictorial form. On the other hand, human cognition and perception must be brought to bear on the graph to decode the information contained therein. If graphical displays are to be effective analytical tools, then this decoding process must work properly. Therefore, it is important to consider some basic principles of graphical information processing.

There now is a voluminous literature on graphical perception covering a variety of different approaches, perspectives, and conclusions (Bertin, 1981, 1983; Cleveland & McGill, 1984a; Kosslyn, 1985, 1989; Simkin & Hastie, 1987; Spence, 1990; Spence & Lewandowsky, 1990). The present discussion is organized around an influential theory developed by Cleveland (1993a). This theory holds that human reception and comprehension of graphical information involves three fundamental perceptual tasks: detection, assembly, and estimation.[2] Let us consider each one of these tasks in turn.

Detection

Cleveland (1993a) defines detection as "the visual recognition of a geometric aspect that encodes a physical value" (p. 328). This means that the basic information from the data must be discernible in the graph. But it also implies that readers' eyes must be drawn to the important information contained within the display rather than to the elements of the graph itself (labels, titles, legends, display grids, etc.). The most general advice on this problem probably is that given by Tufte (1983), who admonishes, "Above all else show the *data*" (p. 92; emphasis added).

Specifically, Tufte (1983) argues that effective graphs strive to maximize the "data-ink ratio," that is, the amount of ink used to depict the "noneras-able core of a graphic" relative to the total amount of ink allocated to the entire graph. Similarly, the data-ink itself should be carefully inspected for redundancies; when found, the latter can be erased to further maximize the amount of unique data information that is contained within each element of the graph. These principles force readers' attention toward the important components of the graph because they tend to eliminate the other, more superfluous elements from appearing in the first place. In so doing, they give primacy to the quantitative information that the graph is intended to convey to its audience.

Assembly

Assembly is the process of discerning patterned regularities among the discrete elements of a graphical display. It serves as a continuation and an extension of the detection process; after recognizing the data themselves, the observer engages in abstraction by moving on to the overall patterns formed by the data—features of the graphical information that transcend the separate data points themselves.

Designing graphical displays to facilitate the assembly process is critical precisely because data points seldom are graphed for their own sake. Instead, the researcher almost always is trying to communicate something about the structure within the data—the shape of a distribution, the relationship between two or more variables, variability across subsets of observations, and so on. Such features can only be conveyed effectively if the graph is constructed in a way that helps the observer combine the separate pictorial elements into a coherent whole.

The assembly process requires that the researcher actively direct readers' attention toward the interesting regularities and patterns of variation that occur in the data. But in so doing, it is important to avoid two problems: (a) overlooking important features contained in the data and (b) imposing patterns that do not really exist or that distort the true variability among the observations.

Estimation

Estimation is "the visual assessment of the relative magnitudes of two or more quantitative physical values" (Cleveland, 1993a, p. 328). Stated differently, estimation focuses on the ability to make accurate magnitude or quantity comparisons across data elements contained within a graph. Human perception does not process all kinds of graphical information with equal levels of accuracy. Therefore, it is important to determine which kinds of geometric constructions lead to the most veridical judgments about perceived magnitudes.

Fortunately, this task is made easier by the fact that human perceptual distortions are systematic rather than random in their biasing effects on judgments about physical phenomena. Therefore, graphical elements can be ranked according to the accuracy of the perceptual judgments that they produce (Cleveland & McGill, 1984a, 1985, 1987). Figure 1.2 shows a series of basic graphical elements, which are arrayed from those that produced the most accurate results at the top left (Figure 1.2A) across the rows and down to those that produced the least accurate judgments at the bottom right (Figure 1.2H). The greatest accuracy in visual perception is obtained when people examine differences between point locations, plotted against a common scale. Judgments are less accurate when points are plotted against identical but nonaligned scales. Information encoded as either the slope of a line segment or an angle between two segments shows quite similar results. Both types of information are less accurate than judgments of line segment lengths but more accurate than judgments based on areas and volumes of figures. Finally, color and shading comparisons produce the least accurate judgments. The conclusion to be drawn from Figure 1.2 is clear-cut: Graphical displays should encode information using geometric elements that fall as close as possible toward the upper end of the hierarchy.

The graphical methods discussed in the remainder of this monograph generally try to optimize all three aspects of graphical perception. In many cases, compromises are necessary. For example, visual *detection* involves the separate data entities in the graph, whereas perceptual *assembly* constructs abstractions from them. Placing emphasis on one of these almost certainly deemphasizes the other. This implies that there usually is no single "best" visualization of a given data set. Therefore, two useful recommendations are as follows. First, always try several different graphical representations of a given data set. Doing so often reveals new and surprising features of the data that otherwise would be missed. Second, recognize that the use of statistical graphics should be an iterative process. Even after deciding on the particular type of graphical display to be used in a given context, it still is important to experiment with the presentation before finalizing it. Seemingly minor changes in the physical features of a graph sometimes can produce major improvements in the amount or type of information that the graph conveys to its readers.

Conclusions

Graphical techniques are important for anyone analyzing empirical data regardless of his or her substantive field. Most of the examples in the statistical graphics literature are taken from the biological and physical sciences involving phenomena such as crop yields, flower petal charac-

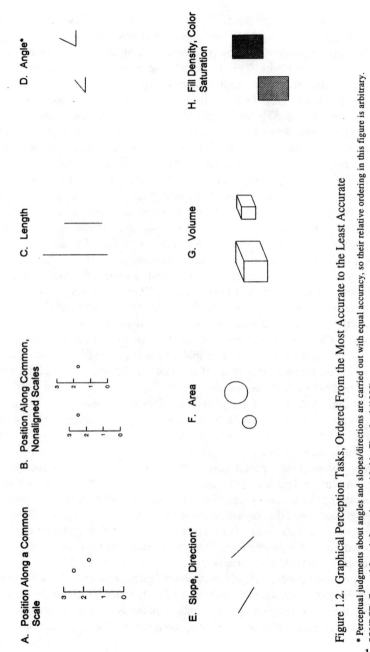

A. Position Along a Common Scale

B. Position Along Common, Nonaligned Scales

C. Length

D. Angle*

E. Slope, Direction*

F. Area

G. Volume

H. Fill Density, Color Saturation

Figure 1.2. Graphical Perception Tasks, Ordered From the Most Accurate to the Least Accurate

* Perceptual judgments about angles and slopes/directions are carried out with equal accuracy, so their relative ordering in this figure is arbitrary.

SOURCE: Created from information provided in Cleveland (1985).

11

teristics, and abrasion loss in various types of rubber. But graphical approaches also should be very useful in the social sciences, where the robustness characteristics of traditional statistical techniques often are pushed to their limits. This is exactly the type of context in which the advantages of statistical graphics can be exploited in very useful ways.

Furthermore, graphically oriented methodologies should be useful for people at varying levels of technical sophistication (Henry, 1995). Beginners gain because effective principles of graphical display for communicating quantitative information can be learned and employed independently of one's level of statistical knowledge. Intermediate-level users should find that graphics provide a natural complement to other ways of learning and using statistics. Advanced practitioners will recognize and understand immediately the fact that graphical approaches represent a different, but complementary, paradigm from more traditional strategies of probabilistic inference. In short, the material discussed in this monograph should be relevant for a very broad audience.

The remainder of the monograph presents a variety of passive graphical displays for univariate and bivariate data. These methods are "passive" in the sense that each involves a single static representation of the data. The objective is to select a view that optimizes the information drawn from the display. Chapter 3 examines methods for visualizing univariate data, and Chapter 4 examines bivariate graphical displays. Finally, a brief concluding chapter recapitulates some of the ideas, principles, and analytic strategies laid out in this monograph.

Graphical displays for multivariate data are covered in a companion volume within this series, *Statistical Graphics for Visualizing Multivariate Data*. Much of that material builds directly on the ideas that are presented in the current volume. The second monograph also introduces active graphical methods: visualizations that rely on real-time interactions between the analyst and the data. The latter are particularly useful for conveying the complexities of multivariate data within the confines of a two-dimensional display medium—usually a computer screen. But active methods also can be helpful for some of the problems encountered with univariate and bivariate data. Thus the contents of these two monographs are closely related to each other.

The monograph on multivariate visualization also contains an appendix that discusses software considerations for statistical graphics. Fortunately, even the most demanding visualization methods are well within the capabilities of most mid-range desktop computers.[3] Thus the hardware and software tools for statistical graphics are widely available within the social science research community. The remaining task is to disseminate information about the graphical techniques themselves. This monograph and its companion volume should make some progress toward that general goal.

2. GRAPHICAL DISPLAYS FOR UNIVARIATE DATA

Univariate graphs provide information about the distribution of observations on a single variable. Like most other statistical methods, a univariate graph is a model. The objective is to construct an abstraction that highlights the salient aspects of the data without distorting any features or imposing undue assumptions. In so doing, a univariate graph is used to overcome the excessive detail contained in the individual data *points* and to provide a useful view of the overall structure contained within the data *set*. In this chapter, I examine several displays that try to achieve these objectives.

Histograms

The histogram is by far the most commonly used procedure for displaying univariate data. It is intended to show the relative concentration (or "density") of observations at all locations across a variable's range of values. More informally, a histogram most often is used to discern the shape of a variable's distribution.

The histogram for a variable, X, is a two-dimensional graph. The horizontal axis (usually) shows the range of X's values. The data density at any specific location within this range, say x_i, is represented by the vertical height of a point plotted at x_i (e.g., Härdle, 1991; Silverman, 1986; Tarter & Kronmal, 1976). If the values of X are relatively continuous (i.e., very few observations share the same data value), then the histogram is constructed by grouping the data into a series of ordered, adjacent, and exhaustive intervals along the variable's range of values; these intervals often are called "bins." All of the bins have a common width of $2h$ units. The density in the range of X values covered by bin j then is defined as the relative concentration of data points that fall within bin j. This density is plotted as a vertical bar, placed at bin j's location along the horizontal axis, with physical width equal to $2h$ and height, y_j, defined by the following formula:

$$y_j = \frac{Number \text{ of } observations \text{ } within in bin \text{ } j}{(2h)n} \qquad (2.1)$$

Note that this function is simply the proportion of observations that fall in bin j multiplied by a factor of $1/(2h)$. The latter term adjusts the height of each bar so that the total area enclosed by the entire histogram is 1.0. After so doing, areas under the histogram can be interpreted as probabilities such that the area covered by each bar can be interpreted as the probability of an observation falling within that bin.

On the other hand, the $1/(2h)$ multiplier simply imposes a uniform shift in the height of the bars, which are themselves measured against an arbitrary vertical axis. Therefore, it often is omitted so that the histogram bar *heights* represent the proportion of observations within each bin. This does not distort the information in any way, and it actually provides additional information that can be interpreted by readers (i.e., the relative frequencies of the intervals corresponding to the bins).

Figure 2.1 presents an example of a histogram, using data on 1986 Medicaid program quality within the 50 states and the District of Columbia. The variable shown in the graph is a summary index created by the Public Citizen Health Research Group (Erdman & Wolfe, 1987); larger values of this variable indicate more effective state Medicaid programs. The bin width has been set to 20 (so $h = 10$), and the leftmost bin starts at 120. From the histogram, it is clear that the distribution is unimodal, centered somewhere between 180 and 200, and that it is asymmetric with a somewhat heavier upper tail. Note that the bars have not been adjusted with the $1/(2h)$ multiplier. Instead, the y_i values given by Equation 2.1 have been multiplied by $100/(2h)$, and so the heights of the bars correspond to the percentages of observations within the bins. The modal interval (again, from 180 to 200) contains about 24% of the states, the lowest interval (i.e., the one from 120 to 140) contains only about 2% of the states, and so on. Thus the histogram provides a great deal of information about the variable's distribution in a very concise manner.

Despite their widespread use, histograms have some serious disadvantages as a mechanism for displaying a variable's distribution (e.g., Chambers et al., 1983; Fox, 1990; Tarter & Kronmal, 1976). The problems stem from the arbitrary nature of the bins used to categorize the continuous data values. Figure 2.2 shows how some seemingly innocuous changes in the bins affect the visual display of the information that is presented in Figure 2.1.

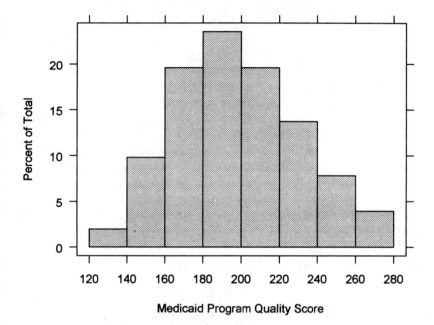

Figure 2.1. Histogram of 1986 Medicaid Program Quality Scores Within the United States
SOURCE: Public Citizen Health Research Group.

First, consider the origin of the bins, that is, the leftmost boundary of the bin enclosing the smallest data values. The origin is specified by the researcher. But its exact location determines the way in which observations are sorted into the bins and thereby affects the shape of the histogram. Figure 2.2A presents an example of this problem. It shows a histogram that is identical to the one shown in Figure 2.1 except for the fact that the origin has been shifted to the right by 5 units, to 125. Apart from that, the data (Medicaid program quality scores) and the bin width ($2h = 20$) remain the same. However, the impression that an observer would receive about the distribution of scores is quite different in each case. Figure 2.1 displays a distribution that is nearly bell shaped with some asymmetry. By contrast, Figure 2.2A shows a distribution containing a more pronounced and nearly rectangular central region along with very sparsely populated upper and

16

A. Bin Origin at 125, Bin Widths of 20.

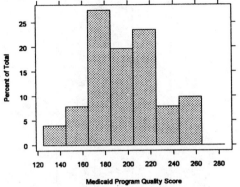

B. Bin Origin at 120, Bin Width of 5.

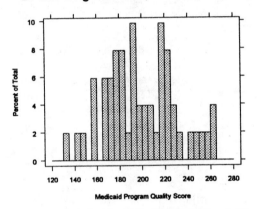

C. Bin Origin at 120, Bin Width of 10.

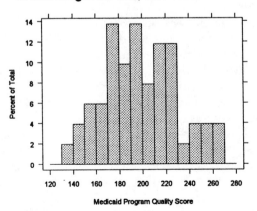

Figure 2.2. Changes in Bin Origin and Bin Widths Affect the Shape of the Histograms

lower tails. The asymmetry, or skewness, is much harder to discern in this display. The alarming thing about the comparison between Figures 2.1 and 2.2A is that their differences arise entirely because of an arbitrary decision—the point of origin for the histogram bins.

A second problem concerns the bin widths. If the value of h is small relative to the range of the data (thereby producing narrow bins), then the histogram will follow the contours of the distribution closely. But the bars also will be affected by random fluctuations in the exact data values. Therefore, the empirical representation of the empirical distribution could be quite "bumpy." Alternatively, wider bins (larger h values) produce a smoother histogram. But they also increase the risk of distorting substantively important features in the variable's distribution. The problem is that wide bins eliminate any possibility of showing local variations in the densities contained within the respective bins. Therefore, the overall shape of the histogram will appear smoother than it should be given the variability in the data.

Figures 2.2B and 2.2C show how the bin widths can influence the shape of a histogram, once again using the Medicaid program quality variable. These two histograms are identical to each other and to the one shown in Figure 2.1 except for the bin widths. Recall that the Figure 2.1 bin widths are 20; they are 5 in Figure 2.2B and 10 in Figure 2.2C. Note how the visual impression of the distribution changes markedly across the different representations of the same data set. Figure 2.2B shows that the distribution of program quality scores actually is bimodal—a potentially important feature of the data that was completely invisible in Figure 2.1. Figure 2.2C shows a "ragged" intermediate shape; the bimodality is less pronounced than it is in Figure 2.2B, and the distribution is beginning to approximate a very rough bell shape. Both of these provide a sharp contrast to the relatively smooth, unimodal, and slightly skewed distribution that is depicted in Figure 2.1. Clearly, the analyst's choice of bin width in a histogram can have a profound impact on the substantive conclusions that are drawn from the graphical display.[4]

Third, the very use of the bins is a distortion of information because any data variability within the bins cannot be displayed in the histogram.[5] At the same time, the discrete nature of the bins generates discontinuities that are manifested visually in the sharp corners of the histogram bars; the latter certainly are not an intrinsic part of the data. Thus the bins that are normally required to construct a histogram almost certainly introduce some degree of inconsistency between the information that actually is displayed and the underlying, presumably continuous variability in the data.

18

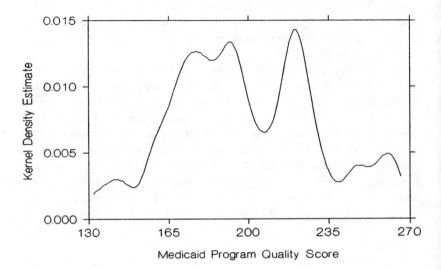

Figure 2.3. Smoothed Histogram of 1986 Medicaid Program Quality Scores
SOURCE: Public Citizen Health Research Group.

Smoothed Histograms

Despite its problems, the general idea behind the histogram remains a good one. As a graphical display, it provides a simple and easily understandable depiction of a univariate distribution. Most of the problems arise in the operationalization rather than in the concept itself. Therefore, statisticians have developed "smoothed histograms," which overcome some of the disadvantages caused by the arbitrary, discrete bins used in traditional histograms (e.g., Härdle, 1991; Silverman, 1986; Tarter & Kronmal, 1976). Specifically, this kind of display tries to show local densities within a distribution as a smooth continuous function of the original continuous data values.[6]

Figure 2.3 presents an example of such a smoothed histogram, using the Medicaid program quality data. This display is interpreted in essentially the same way as a standard histogram. The relative height of the smooth curve corresponds to the local density; the higher the position of the curve, the greater the concentration of data points in that region and vice versa.

The overall height is adjusted so that the total area under the curve is approximately equal to 1.0.[7] Because of this, the area under the curve between any two points along the horizontal scale can be interpreted as the probability that an observation falls within that interval of data values. Note that this display has several potential advantages over the traditional histogram. For one thing, it shows more detail in the variable's distribution. The separate modes clearly are obvious in Figure 2.3, and they are completely absent from the original histogram in Figure 2.1. At the same time, the smooth curve is consistent with the continuous nature of the variable itself; it avoids some of the artificial features imposed by the bins that are required in the standard histogram. Also, the lack of discrete bars in the smoothed histogram makes the overall shape of the distribution more prominent; visual processing of the display is not distracted by sharp variations in bar heights.

Let us examine the logic and general strategy used to create smoothed histograms. Figure 2.4 shows a hypothetical example depicting the major steps of the process. The example uses 10 values of a simulated variable, X, that vary in the interval between 0 and 10.

First, consider Figure 2.4A, which shows the specific observation locations along a number line. The 10 observations are labeled q through z, and their values are 1.1, 2.3, 3.2, 3.7, 4.1, 4.6, 4.9, 5.7, 6.4, and 8.3, respectively. Next, Figure 2.4B depicts each observation as a smooth symmetric distribution centered at the appropriate data value (as we will see, the width of the distributions is determined by the value of h, which is 1.0 in this case). The total area under each of these curves is $1/n$, which represents each observation's contribution to the overall data set.[8]

Now impose m equally spaced points, v_j, along the horizontal axis (i.e., within the potential range of X); these are shown in Figure 2.4C with m set equal to 20 (other values of m also could be used).[9] For each v_j, plot an associated y_j value, which is obtained by summing the heights of the observation distributions that overlap position v_j along the horizontal axis. These plotted points also are shown in Figure 2.4C (the filled circles). Finally, use line segments to connect the plotted points and remove the original data points and observation distributions, as shown in Figure 2.4D. The curve in this figure is called a *density trace* (Chambers et al., 1983), and it can be roughly interpreted as a histogram display of the variable's distribution, albeit one created without initially sorting the observations into discrete bins.[10]

The discussion so far has proceeded intuitively to convey the general idea of a smoothed histogram. The statistical literature more commonly

A. Unidimensional Scatterplot of 10 Data Points

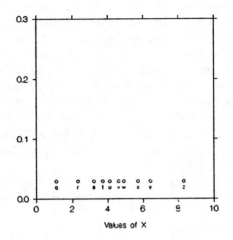

B. Data Points Shown as Kernel Densities

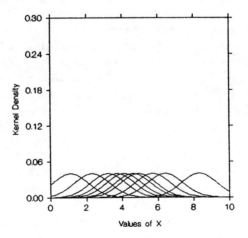

C. Summing Kernel Densities at the 20 v_j

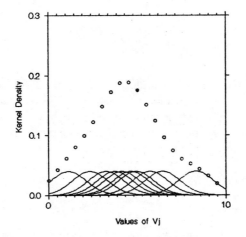

D. Final Smoothed Histogram

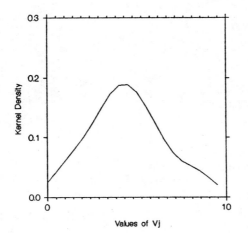

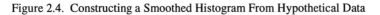

Figure 2.4. Constructing a Smoothed Histogram From Hypothetical Data

represents the latter in terms of a "sliding window" that moves from left to right across the graph, stopping at the successive v_j positions. For each one, the local density, $f(v_j)$, is estimated as a weighted sum of the data as follows:

$$\hat{f}(v_j) = \frac{1}{hn} \sum_{i=1}^{n} K[z_{ij}] \qquad (2.2)$$

On the right-hand side of Equation 2.2, the h and n terms are defined as before, as the window half width (or "bandwidth," as it usually is called in this context) and the sample size, respectively. The z_{ij} represents the distance of an observation from the point at which the density is evaluated, expressed in terms of the bandwidth value, h:

$$z_{ij} = \frac{1}{h}(v_j - x_i) \qquad (2.3)$$

The $K[\bullet]$ term on the right-hand side of Equation 2.2 is a weight function called a *kernel*. This can be any function so long as it integrates to 1.0 and produces values that are unimodal, centered at v_j, and symmetric about v_j. Most kernel functions also produce decreasing values as x_j gets farther away from v_j. Possible kernels include the following:

$$\text{Rectangular: } K_R(z) = \begin{cases} \dfrac{1}{2} & for \ |z| \leq 1.0 \\ 0 & Otherwise \end{cases} \qquad (2.4)$$

$$\text{Triangular: } K_T(z) = \begin{cases} 1 - |z_{ij}| & for \ |z| \leq 1.0 \\ 0 & Otherwise \end{cases} \qquad (2.5)$$

$$\text{Gaussian: } K_G(z) = \frac{1}{\sqrt{2\pi}} e^{-z^2/2} \qquad (2.6)$$

$$\text{Epanechinkov: } K_E(z) = \begin{cases} \dfrac{3}{4\sqrt{5}}\left[1 - \dfrac{z^2}{5}\right] & for \ |z| \leq \sqrt{5} \\ 0 & Otherwise \end{cases} \qquad (2.7)$$

The shapes of these kernel functions are graphed in Figure 2.5. The smoothed histograms shown in Figures 2.3 and 2.4 both are based on the Gaussian kernel, which represents each observation as a normal distribution. However, the choice of a specific kernel seems to have little effect on the final display. To demonstrate this, Figure 2.6 shows alternative smoothed histograms for the Medicaid program quality data, using the rectangular, triangular, Gaussian (this is the same as Figure 2.3), and Epanechinkov kernels, respectively. The shapes of the distributions all are remarkably similar. The jaggedness in the first histogram is due to the sharp corners in the rectangular kernel, whereas the remaining displays are virtually indistinguishable. In practice, it probably is best to limit the choice of kernels to those that decrease symmetrically about the evaluation point (as is the case with the triangular, Gaussian, and Epanechinkov kernels). Substantively, this implies that each observation has the greatest effect at its own specific data value; the observation's contribution to the histogram drops off as one moves away from this value.

Although the specific kernel does not make too much difference, the bandwidth, h, does have an important effect on the shape of the histogram. This value represents the interval over which each observation's contribution is spread along the horizontal axis of the histogram. In the nonrectangular kernels, the h value controls the rate of decrease in an observation's weight as the evaluation point (v_j) gets farther away from the data point (x_i). Stated simply, larger h values always produce smoother histograms. This occurs because as h increases, a larger proportion of the data is contributing to the estimated local density at each evaluation point, v_j. But this in turn obscures the differences between low- and high-density regions within the variable's range.

The smoothed histograms for the Medicaid program quality data shown in Figures 2.3 and 2.6 all are based on an h value of 5. The effects of changing the bandwidth are illustrated in Figure 2.7, which shows several more Gaussian kernel smoothed histograms for the same data. Here, however, the values of h are varied from 5 in the first panel, to 10 in the second, to 15 in the third, and to 20 in the fourth. Note how the narrowest bandwidth produces a relatively "lumpy" histogram, thereby showing a relatively large amount of detail about the variable's distribution. Larger bandwidths, with smoother histograms, make the details disappear and allow the overall shape of the distribution to be discerned more easily.[11]

In statistical terminology, narrow bandwidths produce low-bias, high-variance histograms; the density trace follows the data very closely (low

(text continues on p. 30)

A. Rectangular Kernel

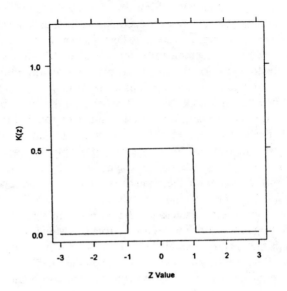

B. Triangular Kernel

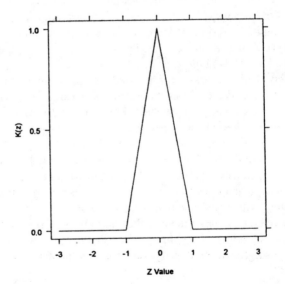

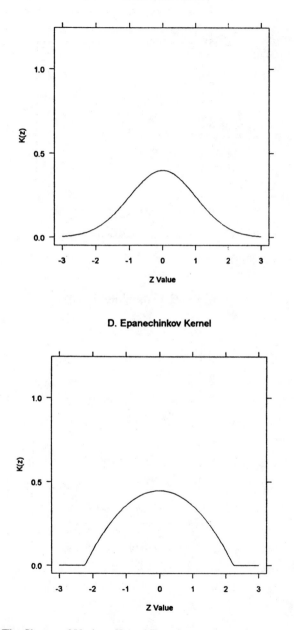

Figure 2.5. The Shapes of Various Kernel Functions

26

A. Rectangular Kernel

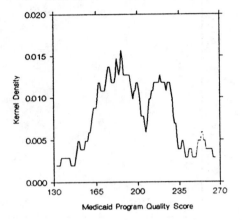

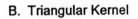

B. Triangular Kernel

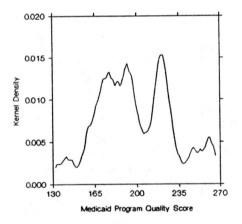

C. Gaussian Kernel

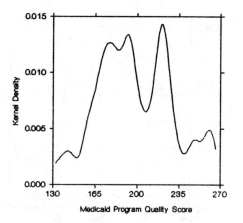

D. Epanechinkov Kernel

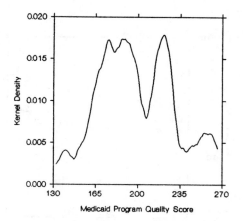

Figure 2.6. Smoothed Histograms of Medicaid Program Quality Scores Created With Different Kernel Density Functions

A. Bandwidth h = 5

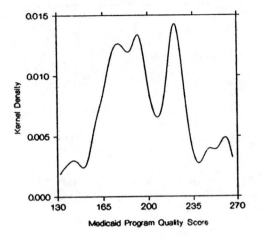

B. Bandwidth, h = 10

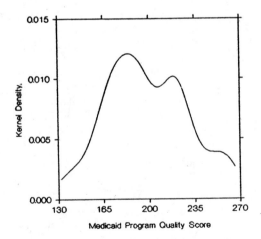

C. Bandwidth, *h* = 15

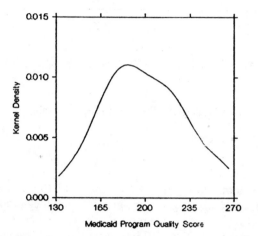

D. Bandwidth, *h* = 20

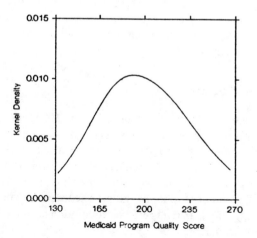

Figure 2.7. Changing the Bandwidth on Smoothed Histograms of Medicaid Program Quality Data
SOURCE: Public Citizen Health Research Group.

30

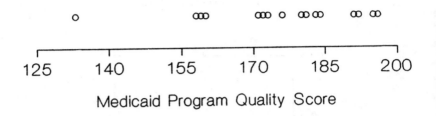

Figure 2.8. Univariate Scatterplot of Medicaid Program Quality Scores for Southern States
SOURCE: Public Citizen Health Research Group.

bias), but the smooth curve jumps around quite a bit (high variance). Larger bandwidths are high bias and low variance because they produce a smooth density trace (low variance in the plotted values) but depart from the actual data to a more substantial degree (high bias in the graphical representation). In practice, the selection of a specific bandwidth for a smoothed histogram always involves a trade-off between these two considerations.[12]

Smoothed histograms avoid some of the problems that are encountered with traditional histograms. However, their final form still is affected by two relatively arbitrary decisions about the bandwidth and (to a lesser extent) the specific kernel weighting function. The alternative univariate displays considered in the remaining sections of this chapter eliminate these problems entirely by graphing the data points (or some function of those points) directly.

Unidimensional Scatterplots

A unidimensional scatterplot (Chambers et al., 1983) simply shows each observation as a point plotted along a scale line that represents the range of data values. Figure 2.8 shows a unidimensional scatterplot of Medicaid program quality scores for 16 southern states. This type of graph can convey a great deal of information without the potential loss of information or distortion encountered in a histogram. The main drawback of a unidimensional scatterplot is that it is effectively limited to small data sets. With large numbers of observations, there is a great deal of overplotting. This makes it difficult to discern individual observations and concentrations of

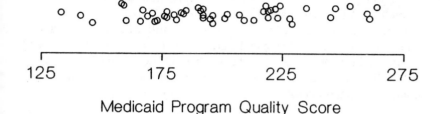

Figure 2.9. Univariate Scatterplot of Medicaid Program Quality Scores Including All States and District of Columbia
NOTE: Points are jittered.
SOURCE: Public Citizen Health Research Group.

data points within the overall distribution. In fact, this is why Figure 2.8 contains only a fraction of the full set of 51 Medicaid program quality scores.

There are two general and mutually supportive strategies for minimizing the effects of overplotting. First, it is important to select a plotting symbol that allows readers to detect overplotted points. The relatively large open circles in Figure 2.8 are effective for this purpose. Small and/or solid points would coalesce into incomprehensible blobs within the display. Similarly, if the plotting symbols had straight sides (e.g., squares, diamonds), then it would be much more difficult to separate them visually into individual data points when they overlap within the display.

Second, the overplotting can be reduced by displacing the points somewhat in the direction perpendicular to the variable's scale line. This process is called *jittering* (Chambers et al., 1983). Each observation is assigned a random number generated from a uniform distribution over some arbitrary but small interval. This number then is plotted on the vertical axis (with the original variable still plotted on the horizontal) to separate the points and facilitate visual inspection. Figure 2.9 shows a jittered unidimensional scatterplot of the Medicaid program quality variable for all 51 observations. Each state has been assigned a random number in the interval from −0.5 to +0.5, and this is used to locate the data points along the vertical axis.[13] Note how the bimodal nature of this distribution can be discerned from the relatively dense point clouds in the intervals around 175 to 200 and around 200 to 225 on the horizontal axis.

In a jittered unidimensional scatterplot, it is important to keep the range of the random variation small relative to the variation in the substantive variable. This means that the plotted points still will be confined to a relatively small physical area in the graph (i.e., the point cloud is enclosed within a narrow "band"). When the number of observations is large, there still will be quite a bit of overplotting despite the jittering. Therefore, unidimensional scatterplots remain primarily useful for small data sets.

Quantile Plots

A quantile plot is a visual display that provides a great deal of quite detailed information about a univariate distribution (e.g., Chambers et al., 1983; Gnanadesikan, 1977; Wilk and Gnanadesikan, 1968). The quantiles of a distribution are a set of summary statistics that locate relative positions within the complete ordered array of data values. Specifically, the pth quantile of a distribution, X, is defined as the value x_p, such that approximately $100p\%$ of the empirical observations have lower values than x_p.

The empirical quantiles for a variable, X, are obtained as follows. First, sort the data so that the n observations are arrayed from the smallest value, $x_{(1)}$, to the largest, $x_{(n)}$. The parentheses in the subscript denote position within the *sorted* collection of data values. The quantile corresponding to any observation within this sorted distribution, say $x_{(i)}$, usually is obtained as follows:

$$p_i = \frac{i - 0.5}{n} \tag{2.8}$$

In Equation 2.8, the quantity 0.5 is subtracted from each i value in the numerator to avoid extreme quantiles of exactly 0 or 1. The latter would cause problems if empirical quantiles were to be compared against quantiles derived from a theoretical, asymptotic distribution such as the normal. This adjustment has no effect on the shape of any graphical displays that use the quantiles.

In the quantile plot, each observation, i, is shown as a point in a two-dimensional graph. The vertical coordinate for i is the data value, x_i, and the horizontal coordinate is the corresponding quantile value, p_i. All quantile plots contain a monotonically increasing array of points; this is the *empirical cumulative distribution function* (ECDF) for the plotted variable. The local slopes that occur within segments of the ECDF provide information about the features of the variable's distribution. Specifically, a flat section (or very shallow slope) in the quantile plot signals a relatively high concentration of data points within that interval of the variable's distribution. Conversely, a nearly vertical or steeply sloped section within the quantile plot corresponds to a low-density area of the empirical distribution.

Figure 2.10 shows a few hypothetical examples that demonstrate how the shape of a variable's distribution is reflected in the specific nature of the monotonic ECDF in the quantile plot. There are six separate sections in the figure. Each one contains simulated data on 200 observations drawn from differently shaped distributions. In each section, the panel on the left shows a histogram of the data, whereas the panel on the right shows the corresponding quantile plot. First, consider the uniform distribution contained in Figure 2.10A. The density of the points is constant across the range of values, so the quantile plot is linear. Next, Figure 2.10B shows that a symmetric, bell-shaped distribution produces a quantile plot shaped like a "transposed S." Here the strong central mode is signaled by the relatively flat array of points around the center of the quantile plot. The tails of the distribution are shown by the more vertical segments that occur in the leftmost and rightmost areas of the quantile plot. The two skewed distributions in Figures 2.10C and 2.10D both produce quantile plots with a single bend; the curve bends upward for positive skew and downward for negative skew. This occurs because the segment of the ECDF containing the steep slope corresponds to the tail of the distribution; of course, this falls to the right with positive skewness and toward the left with negative skewness. The bimodal distribution in Figure 2.10E generates the quantile plot with two flat sections. Also, note the "gap" that occurs in the vertical section of the point array; this corresponds to the interval between the two modes of the distribution, where data points are sparse. Finally, the short-tailed distribution in the last section of Figure 2.10 produces a relatively "shallow" transposed S shape, something in between the quantile plots for the uniform and bell-shaped distributions depicted earlier in the figure. With some practice, quantile plots can be used just like histograms to obtain information about the shape of a univariate distribution (Hoaglin, 1985).

Let us construct a quantile plot using some real data. Table 2.1 shows the empirical quantiles for the Medicaid program quality variable. The leftmost column shows the states, the next column gives the i values, and the third column contains the sorted $x_{(i)}$ values for all 51 observations. The corresponding quantiles, the p_i's, are shown in the rightmost column. The

A. Uniform Distribution

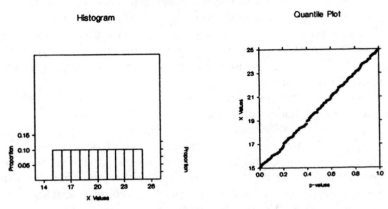

Histogram

Quantile Plot

B. Symmetric, Bell-Shaped Distribution

Histogram

Quantile Plot

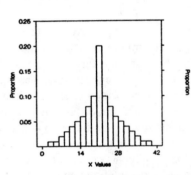

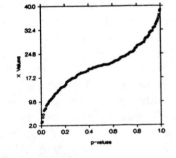

C. Positively Skewed Distribution

Histogram

Quantile Plot

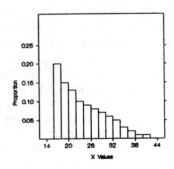

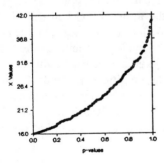

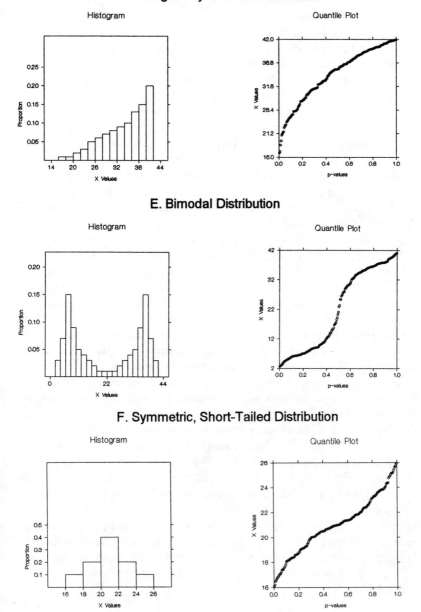

Figure 2.10. Comparison of Histograms and Quantile Plots for Differently Shaped Data Distributions

quantile plot based on this information is shown in Figure 2.11. The bimodality in the distribution of Medicaid program quality scores is indicated by the two separate, relatively "flat" sections within the graph. One of these is the shallow-sloped area that occurs from approximately the 0.4 quantile to the 0.55 quantile; this corresponds to a fairly narrow band of X values around 190. The second relatively flat area in the graph falls in the interval between the 0.7 and 0.8 quantiles (X values from about 215 to 220). At the same time, there are relatively steep segments at both the upper and lower ends of the quantile plot, with the former containing a few more points than the latter. These features correspond to the two asymmetric tails of the empirical distribution of scores.

Along with the distributional shape, the quantile plot can be used to obtain a visual estimate of certain summary statistics for the variable in the graph. For example, the median is an important order statistic, measuring the center of the variable's values. The median also corresponds to the 0.5 quantile. In Figure 2.11, the 0.5 position can be located along the horizontal axis; the height of the ECDF at this position coincides with a value of about 190 on the vertical axis, and this provides an easy estimate of the median for this variable (the actual value of the median is very close to this, at 195).[14] Similarly, the first and third quartiles of a distribution are the 0.25 and 0.75 quantiles. Just as with the median, these points can be located on the horizontal axis and used to estimate the corresponding x_p values. In this case, $x_{.25}$ falls at about 170 and $x_{.75}$ is approximately 225 (the actual values are 176 and 222 for the first and third quartiles, respectively).

In summary, quantile plots provide a great deal of information. They also overcome some of the disadvantages associated with the other kinds of displays considered so far. Unlike histograms, quantile plots show all of the data, and so there are no problems associated with arbitrary bins or bandwidths. Unlike univariate scatterplots, overplotting is not really a problem with a quantile plot. It is the shape of the monotonic array rather than the locations of the individual plotting symbols that provides the useful information about the distribution. Accordingly, quantile plots can be used for data sets of virtually any size. And, as we have just seen, the information contained within a quantile plot can be very easily related to several important summary statistics; thus it facilitates the "translation" between graphical and numeric representations of quantitative information. For all of these reasons, quantile plots are useful tools for visualizing univariate data.

TABLE 2.1
Quantiles From the Distribution of
1986 Medicaid Program Quality Scores

State	Position Within Ordered Data (i)	Program Quality Scores $X_{(i)}$	p Values $p_i = (i - .5) / 51$
Minnesota	51	264	.990
Wisconsin	50	261	.971
New York	49	260	.951
Massachusetts	48	253	.931
Connecticut	47	247	.912
California	46	245	.892
New Jersey	45	235	.873
Washington	44	229	.853
Oregon	43	228	.833
Michigan	42	224	.814
District of Columbia	41	223	.794
Maine	40	222	.775
Iowa	39	222	.755
Maryland	38	220	.735
Vermont	37	219	.716
Rhode Island	36	219	.696
Hawaii	35	218	.676
Illinois	34	217	.657
Pennsylvania	33	213	.637
Nebraska	32	209	.618
Kansas	31	207	.598
Utah	30	202	.578
Montana	29	201	.559
Kentucky	28	196	.539
Colorado	27	196	.520
Georgia	26	195	.500
West Virginia	25	192	.480
Ohio	24	192	.461
Indiana	23	192	.441
Florida	22	191	.422
North Dakota	21	190	.402
Alaska	20	185	.382
Delaware	19	184	.363
South Carolina	18	183	.343
Tennessee	17	181	.324
North Carolina	16	180	.304
New Mexico	15	177	.284

(continued)

38

TABLE 2.1 Continued

State	Position Within Ordered Data (i)	Program Quality Scores $X_{(i)}$	p Values $p_i = (i - .5) / 51$
New Hampshire	14	177	.265
Lousiana	13	176	.245
Texas	12	173	.225
Oklahoma	11	172	.206
Virginia	10	171	.186
Idaho	9	169	.167
Nevada	8	167	.147
South Dakota	7	166	.127
Akansas	6	160	.108
Missouri	5	159	.088
Alabama	4	158	.069
Arizona	3	146	.049
Wyoming	2	141	.029
Mississippi	1	133	.010

SOURCE: Public Citizen Health Research Group.

Box Plots

As just explained, a quantile plot shows all of the data. Sometimes, however, this degree of detail really is not necessary in a graphical display (Cleveland, 1993b). When that is the case, a box plot (sometimes called a "box-and-whisker diagram") provides an extremely useful alternative (Hartwig & Dearing, 1979; Tukey, 1977).

Box plots still are based on the quantiles of a distribution, but they focus directly on what might be considered the "most important" quantiles—the *quartiles*, or the 0.25, 0.5, and 0.75 quantiles. These divide the overall distribution into four equally filled intervals. As a concrete example, Figure 2.12 shows the box plot for the Medicaid program quality variable. The display is placed parallel to a scale line representing the variable's range of values; this can be oriented in either a horizontal or a vertical direction. Here the figure shows a vertical box plot.

The lower and upper horizontal edges of the box are located at the first and third quartiles of the data, respectively; therefore, the height of the box corresponds directly to the interquartile range (IQR) of the distribution. The horizontal line within the interior of the box is placed at the vertical scale position corresponding to the median value. The vertical lines (or "whiskers") above and below the central box require some intermediate calculations. First, define two values (called the "inner fences") as follows:

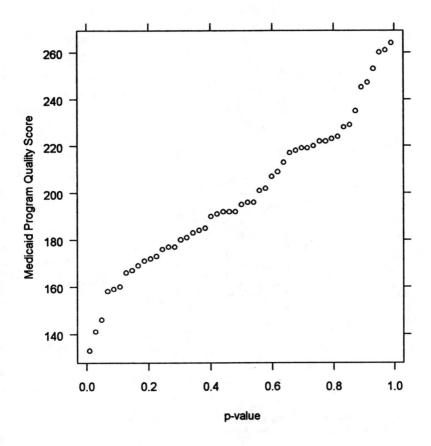

Figure 2.11. Quantile Plot of 1986 Medicaid Program Quality Scores
SOURCE: Public Citizen Health Research Group.

| Lower Inner Fence: | $x_{.25} - 1.5\ IQR$ |
| Upper Inner Fence: | $x_{.75} + 1.5\ IQR$ |

Note that these fences are "imaginary values" that usually do not occur within the empirical data. They are used to obtain the upper and lower "adjacent values," which are defined as the two most extreme empirical data values that fall within the respective inner fences. Lines called whiskers are extended from the lower and upper edges of the box out to the lower and upper adjacent values.

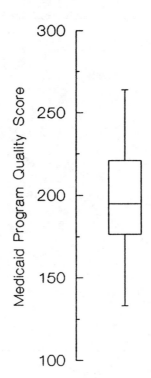

Figure 2.12. Box Plot of 1986 Medicaid Program Quality Scores
SOURCE: Public Citizen Health Research Group.

In Figure 2.12, the adjacent values correspond to the minimum and maximum values within the data set, and so the box plot is complete. Note that the median line in Figure 2.12 is off-center within the box; it is closer to the lower quartile than it is to the upper quartile. This shows that the central portion of the variable's distribution contains an asymmetric density of data points; observations are more spread out above the median than they are below the median. On the other hand, the two whisker lines are of approximately equal length, showing that neither tail of the distribution is markedly longer than the other.

It is useful to compare this display to Figures 2.1, 2.3, 2.7, and 2.11 to see how the information provided by a box plot differs from that shown in a histogram, a smoothed histogram, or a quantile plot of the same data. The information about the tails of the distribution seems to be consistent across the different depictions; in each case, the most extreme subsets of data points at the upper and lower ends of the distribution are relatively symmetric and similarly sized. But some potentially important differences emerge in the information provided about the central subset of data values. Stated simply, the box plot does not show the separate modes that were plainly obvious in the first smoothed histogram (Figure 2.3) and the quantile plot (Figure 2.11) of these data. The box plot merely *summarizes* the distribution and, in so doing, necessarily overlooks some of the detail within the data points. But this does not necessarily mean that the box plot gives an *inaccurate* portrayal of the data. On the contrary, Figure 2.12 reveals the asymmetry in the central region of the distribution, and this is perfectly consistent with the histogram in Figure 2.1 and the smoothed histogram in Figure 2.7C. Recall that the latter used a relatively wide bandwidth to construct the density trace; therefore, it too provides a relatively broad undetailed depiction of the distribution. The differences between the box plot and the other graphs exemplify some of the trade-offs that must be weighed when considering what kind of univariate graph to use on a particular data set.

The box plot of the Medicaid quality data is particularly simple because data points do not extend beyond the adjacent values. However, this will not always be the case. If there are any observations beyond the adjacent values, then they are called "outside values" and are shown as individual points in the display. The plotting symbols for outside values are located at their respective positions on the scale line, along an imaginary line extending from the whiskers. Figure 2.13 shows another box plot to illustrate the use of outside values. Here the data are 1992 public education expenditures within the United States. Even a quick glance at the box plot shows that the distribution is skewed positive. The distance from the median to the third quartile (i.e., the top edge of the box) is about double that from the median to the first quartile (the lower edge of the box). The upper whisker also is much longer than the lower one. Clearly, the upper 50% of the observations in this distribution are spread across a wider range of values than are the lower 50%. But even after we take the overall skewness into account, there remain three outside values on the upper side of the distribution; these indicate states with unusually high education expenditures. Note that there actually are two types of outside values. *Mild* outside values are shown in the figure as asterisks; they fall beyond the inner fences but within the *outer* fences, which are defined as

42

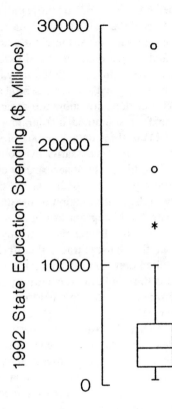

Figure 2.13. Box Plot of 1992 Public Education Expenditures in the United States
SOURCE: Public Citizen Health Research Group.

Lower Outer Fence: $x_{.25} - 3\,IQR$
Upper Outer Fence: $x_{.75} + 3\,IQR$

Extreme outside values are shown as open circles and are defined as any points that occur beyond the outer fences. Figure 2.13 shows one mild outside value and two extreme outside values.

By their very nature, outside values (whether mild or extreme) represent unusual observations. There will be very few outside values within any univariate distribution, and so there usually is no problem graphing them individually within the box plot. It is important to do so to identify unusual and/or problematic aspects of the data. At the very least, the presence of outside values should lead the analyst to inspect these observations more closely. In this case, the mild outside value is Texas, whereas the more extreme observations are New York and California. These all are large states with heavy population concentrations in urban areas. This common feature suggests that it might be useful to adjust the education expenditure figures by state size before subjecting them to any further analyses. Of course, unusual observations can be discerned in the other univariate graphical displays. But their distinctive pictorial representation in the box plot really emphasizes their differences from the rest of the distribution and thereby encourages further investigation.

In summary, box plots show several important properties of a univariate distribution. The median line locates a robust estimate of the distribution's center. The width of the box corresponds directly to the degree of spread or variability in the values. The distribution's symmetry is indicated by the relative distances from the median line to the upper and lower edges of the box and also by the relative sizes of the two whiskers.

More generally, the box plot operationalizes several terms that often are used in informal discussions of univariate data (Mosteller & Tukey, 1977). The box shows the central region of the distribution, the whiskers are the tails, and the outside values represent any outliers that may exist in the data. The only real drawback of a box plot is that it is fairly insensitive to multiple modes within the data. But beyond this limitation, the box plot crams a great deal of information into a concise and easily understood visual display. Because of this, it probably is the second most frequently used graphical method for univariate data, behind only the histogram in popularity.[15]

Dot Plots

A dot plot (also called an index plot) is a useful display method whenever data values are associated with identifying information such as a label or an index number. Dot plots are useful in a variety of situations, and there are several different versions of the basic display (Cleveland, 1984). Their common features are as follows. One axis of the dot plot (usually the horizontal) represents the scale for the variable under investigation. The other axis (usually the vertical) contains rows that provide a label or an index for each data value. Observations are sorted according to the values of the variable under investigation and then plotted as points at the appropriate scale location within each row. In this manner, the dot plot identifies both the specific data points and the numeric values that are associated with them.

Figure 2.14 shows a dot plot of the Medicaid program quality scores. The information in the graph is easy to interpret. The labels in the margin of the vertical axis are two-letter state name abbreviations. The quality score for each state's Medicaid program can be determined by examining the location of the plotted point within that row; the farther the point is to the right, the better the measured quality of the program, and vice versa.

The dot plot is effectively the same as a transposed quantile plot, and the shape of the point array can be interpreted in a manner similar to those displays. Once again, the local density of the distribution is reflected in the local slope of the plotted points. In this case, however, the slopes are interpreted in exactly the opposite way from the earlier discussion (because of the transposition). Here a steep or nearly vertical array of points indicates a dense segment of the variable's distribution. Conversely, a shallow slope along a sequence of points indicates an area containing few observations within the distribution. In Figure 2.14, we once again can see the two modes of the distribution (corresponding to the nearly vertical sections in the point array) and the asymmetric tails (in the long and fairly steep point array in the lower left side of the graph and the shorter, shallower string of points near the upper right-hand corner).

The dot plot also facilitates the identification of particular state locations within the overall distribution. The horizontal lines extending across each row of the graph facilitate table look-up, that is, the ability to connect individual data values with labels. For example, Figure 2.14 makes it easy to see that Georgia falls at the exact center of the distribution (26th within the total n of 51); its Medicaid program quality score of 195 also is the median value for the distribution. Similarly, Minnesota and Mississippi can be identified as the states with the best and worst programs, respectively. In short, the dot plot succinctly provides a great deal of information about both a variable's distribution and the specific observations within the data. Because of this, it is perhaps useful to think of the dot plot as a visual display that stands somewhere in between the concrete details contained in the raw data and the abstract models provided by the other univariate graphical methods.

Dot plots also can be used very effectively to display summaries of data values within aggregate units. For example, Figure 2.15 shows the median

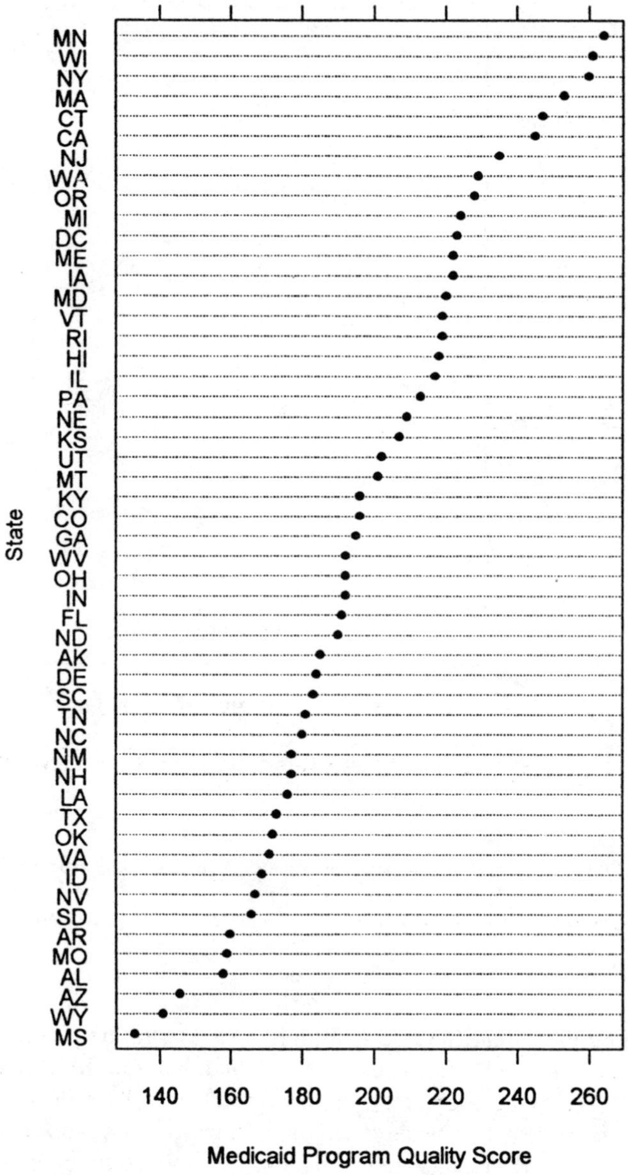

Figure 2.14. Dot Plot of State Medicaid Program Quality Scores
SOURCE: Public Citizen Health Research Group.

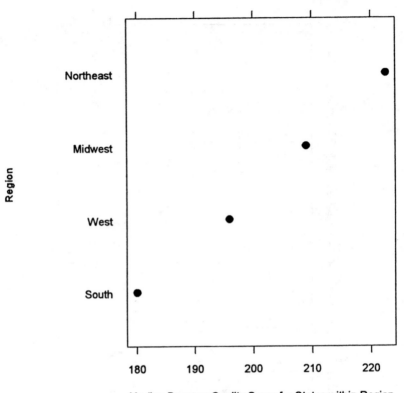

Figure 2.15. Dot Plot of Median State Medicaid Program Quality Scores Within Regions of the United States
SOURCE: Public Citizen Health Research Group.

Medicaid program quality scores within four regions of the United States. Because there are only four distinct values (and therefore little chance of serious table look-up problems), the horizontal lines have been omitted from the interior of the display. This maximizes the data-ink ratio and produces a "cleaner" graphical representation of the quantitative information.

It probably is accurate to say that dot plots are not very well known to most researchers. This is unfortunate because they have some distinct advantages over their major "competitors" for displaying labeled data: pie charts and bar charts. One of these advantages is practical in nature. Dot plots can show a larger number of data values than can either pie charts or bar charts. For example, a pie chart with anything more than a small handful of "wedges" is virtually impossible to interpret through visual inspection. With bar charts, the widths of the bars necessarily decrease as the number of distinct data points increases. In principle, this process could continue indefinitely until the bars become lines. But in that case, the display is in effect a type of dot plot. Of course, there still is an upper bound to the number of data values/labels that can be shown effectively in a dot plot; this number is likely to be relatively small in absolute size. But it definitely is safe to say that dot plots can incorporate more distinct components (i.e., either observations or aggregated units) than can the other methods for displaying labeled data.

These practical comparisons are important, but there are other theory-based reasons for using dot plots to display labeled data (Cleveland, 1994). Consider the visual processing tasks that are required to interpret the graphical information. The dot plot involves comparisons of point locations along a common scale. As explained in Chapter 1, this is a graphical processing task that human observers can carry out quite accurately. By contrast, pie charts require analysts to make comparisons between the angles, arcs, and/or areas that define the sizes of the pie wedges. All of these judgments fall at relatively low positions within Cleveland's hierarchy of visual processing tasks. Thus there is strong evidence that dot plots will lead to more accurate estimation of relative quantitative values than will pie charts.

Like dot plots, bar charts also require judgments about locations along a common scale, but they often are affected adversely by a different problem. Consider Figure 2.16A, which shows a bar chart of the regional median values on the Medicaid program quality variable—in other words, the same information shown in the dot plot of Figure 2.15. Cleveland (1984, 1994) argues that people tend to interpret the *areas* blocked off within the respective bars. But this is inappropriate in the present case because the bottoms of the bars are anchored at the completely arbitrary value of 170. As a result, it is just not meaningful to interpret the lengths of the bars as if they were providing any information about the relative magnitudes of the data values across the observational units. It would be valid to do so only if the bars were anchored at a meaningful zero point. But even if that were possible with these data, Figure 2.16B shows that this still would create a problematic graphical display. The distance from the zero point to the minimum bar length (180 units) is much larger than the variability among the bar lengths themselves (which range over only about 42 units, from 180.0 to 222.5). Because of this, the visual resolution of the differences between the separate data values is hampered. When the ends of the bars are squeezed into the right side of the display, it is much more difficult to discern how much the lengths change from one bar to the next.

A properly constructed dot plot avoids these problems. In fact, this is exactly why the horizontal lines were extended all the way across the display in Figure 2.14. The lines within the rows all have equal lengths, and so they do not supply any visual cues that would encourage observers to make inappropriate judgments about the relative sizes of data values. Similar reasoning applies when the horizontal lines are omitted entirely, as they were from the dot plot in Figure 2.16. In either case, the dot plot downplays magnitude comparisons, and the scale values in the display can be set to facilitate visual perception of the *differences* between the data values.

Of course, there are situations in which magnitude comparisons of data values are appropriate. In such cases, the dot plot can be adapted to provide an effective graphical display. Figure 2.17 shows a dot plot of 1992 per capita social welfare expenditures within the United States. The data values represent ratio-level measurements, so they have a meaningful zero point and magnitude comparisons are legitimate and meaningful. In recognition of this fact, the dot plot shows lines that extend from the zero point on the scale line out to each of the plotted data points. The lines still could have been extended across the full scale or even omitted entirely. However, this version produces a higher data-ink ratio than do full-length lines and still facilitates table look-up. Once again, it is reasonable to think in terms of ratios of the data values, so magnitude comparisons of the line lengths are fully appropriate.

In summary, dot plots are excellent graphical displays for labeled uni-variate data. They contain a great deal of information, are easy to interpret, and overcome a number of the problems associated with other kinds of displays. For these reasons, they probably should be used frequently in empirical research.

Conclusions

When dealing with univariate data, researchers often have difficulty seeing the forest (i.e., a variable's distribution) because of the trees that it contains (i.e., the individual observations). Univariate graphical displays

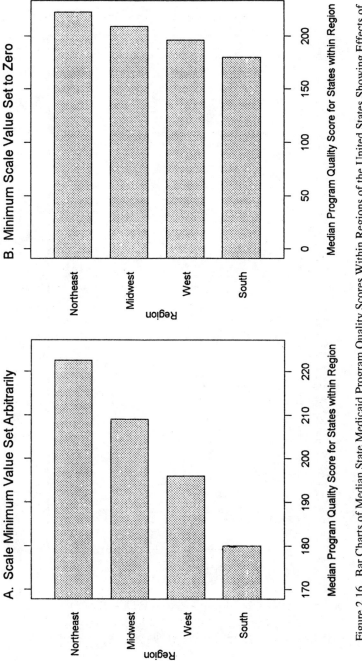

Figure 2.16. Bar Charts of Median State Medicaid Program Quality Scores Within Regions of the United States Showing Effects of Scale Limits on Visual Perception

SOURCE: Public Citizen Health Research Group.

49

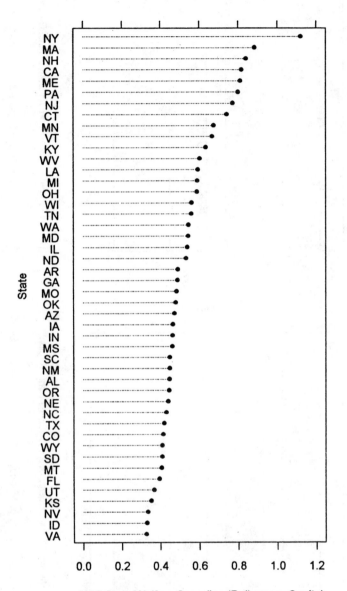

Figure 2.17. Dot Plot Showing 1992 Social Welfare Expenditures in the United States
SOURCE: *1993 Statisical Abstract of the United States.*

are intended to help us discern the forest without distorting or omitting any of the relevant information contributed by the individual trees. This chapter has presented a broad survey of tools for achieving these objectives.

The material presented in this chapter raises an obvious question: How does one decide which kind of display should be used in any specific data analysis situation? The answer to this question will be based, in part, on relatively subjective factors (the researcher's aesthetic sense, available software, space for presentation, etc.). But it is also important to keep theoretical principles in mind while selecting a graphical method. Accordingly, univariate displays can be evaluated in terms of Cleveland's model of visual perception, which was introduced in Chapter 1. For example, univariate scatterplots and dot plots are particularly suitable for *detection* or for the ability to discern individual data points in the graph. On the other hand, smoothed histograms and quantile plots probably are better for *assembly*, the ability to extract relatively unambiguous information about the nature and shape of the variable's distribution. And *estimation*, the degree to which the graphical information can be used to obtain specific values for data points and/or descriptive statistics, is facilitated in graphs such as dot plots and box plots. The researcher must balance these three different (and sometimes conflicting) considerations while selecting a graphical display for any given data analysis context.

Of course, it is impossible to say that any particular graphical method is the single overall "best" one given that these displays are used for many different purposes. Nevertheless, it is hard to overlook the fact that some of the more familiar kinds of graphs (particularly histograms) seem to have more disadvantages than do other less well-known types (particularly quantile and dot plots). At the same time, however, readers must be able to understand the information contained in a graph. The fact remains that histograms are more widely recognized than quantile plots. Therefore, they probably will remain the "workhorse" univariate graphical display for the foreseeable future.

3. GRAPHICAL DISPLAYS FOR BIVARIATE DATA

Bivariate data are ubiquitous in all fields of scientific research. They consist of paired measurements on two quantitative variables, say X and Y. That is, each observation, i, in a data set containing n observations possesses numerical values x_i and y_i. Bivariate data are commonly used to examine the relationship between two variables or the functional dependence of one variable (usually *Y*) on the other (usually *X*). The basic visualization tool for this purpose is the familiar two-dimensional scatterplot (Cleveland & McGill, 1984b). Of course, scatterplots are very widely recognized. Still, it is worthwhile to describe briefly their basic components as well as some general principles to guide their construction.

Definition and Construction Guidelines for Bivariate Scatterplots

The scatterplot is a rectangular, two-dimensional graphical display that illustrates the joint distribution of values on two variables. It is constructed from two perpendicular coordinate axes that form the *scale rectangle* for the graph. Each axis can be thought of as a number line, calibrated in the data units of one of the variables. Tick marks on the axes are used to identify data values, and the tick marks along each axis generally encompass the extremes (and hence the range) of the observed data values for that variable. Observations are plotted as points within the interior of the scatterplot. It is useful to think of the points as being plotted within a *data rectangle*; the latter is an imaginary region (i.e., it is invisible in the graph) that just encloses the data points. Each point's position is determined by the intersection of the perpendicular projections from that observation's coordinates along the two axes.

Cleveland (1994) provides some general principles that should be followed when constructing scatterplots.[16] A partial list of these ideas includes the following.

Make sure that the plotting symbols are visually prominent and relatively resistant to overplotting effects. This is important to facilitate visual detection of the basic data contained within the scatterplot. For example, small plotting symbols are easily overlooked. At the same time, larger filled symbols make it quite difficult to distinguish overlapping data points. For these reasons, open circles make good general-purpose plotting symbols for bivariate scatterplots.

Rectangular grid lines usually are unnecessary within the scale rectangle of a scatterplot. Table look-up (identifying the variable values associated with a particular data point) can be accomplished with the scale lines alone. Therefore, additional grid lines just reduce the data-ink ratio without providing much in the way of useful information. In so doing, they may have an adverse effect on both the detection and assembly aspects of visual perception.

The data rectangle should be slightly smaller than the scale rectangle of the scatterplot. Otherwise, it is likely that some data will be hidden as a result of intersections between points and the scale lines. Obviously, this is detrimental to the process of visual detection.

Tick marks should point outward, rather than inward, from the scale lines. Moving the ticks outside the scale rectangle further reduces the possibility of collisions between data points and other elements of the scatter diagram. Therefore, this provides another enhancement to visual detection in the scatterplot.

Relatively few tick marks should be used on each axis. As explained in Chapter 1, graphs are not very effective for gauging precise numerical values in data. More general informal estimation of quantitative information can be carried out through simple visual projection from the plotted points back to the scale axes. Excess tick marks add little to the accuracy of this process; therefore, they unnecessarily reduce the data-ink ratio within the graph.

If necessary, transform the data values (or, alternatively, use transformed scales on the axes of the graph) so that the plotted points fill up as much of the data rectangle as possible. Outlying observations and asymmetric univariate distributions can ruin visual resolution of the information in a scatterplot because the bulk of the plotted points may be forced into a small subset of the overall data rectangle. Applying an appropriate power transformation (e.g., raise data values to a power smaller than 1 to correct for high-end outliers and positive skewness, use powers larger than 1 to deal with low-end outliers and negative skewness) will spread out the plotted points and facilitate the process of visual assembly in the graphical display.[17] In other words, patterns and structure within the data will be more readily discernible.

Most of the preceding guidelines probably appear to be simple and intuitive common sense. However, even a cursory inspection of the research literature in almost any substantive field reveals how frequently these principles are violated when scatterplots are employed in empirical social research.

Consider the two scatterplots shown in Figure 3.1. Both of these displays illustrate the relationship between the size of the 1986 Medicaid recipient population within each state and total state Medicaid program expenditures in 1986. However, the first scatterplot (Figure 3.1A) violates all of the preceding guidelines. The points are very small, the scale lines coincide with the maximum and minimum data values, there is a background grid based on a large number of tick marks (which themselves point inward), and extreme skewness and outliers in both variables' distributions force most of the points into the lower left-hand corner of the scale rectangle. Data points are hidden by other elements of the scatterplot, and it is very difficult to discern any pattern or structure among the plotted points. This graph is largely useless for learning anything about the relationship between Medicaid recipient populations and program expenditures within the Uniated States.

Now consider Figure 3.1B, which corrects all of the problems from the preceding display. In this scatterplot, the points are visually prominent open circles, the data rectangle is made smaller than the scale rectangle, the grid has been omitted, the number of ticks has been reduced, the tick marks themselves are pointing outward, and logarithmic scales (Base 2) are used on the axes. The net effect of these changes is immediately obvious. All of the data now can be detected through visual inspection; furthermore, it is easy to assemble the separate points into a general pattern. This scatterplot reveals the existence of a strong linear relationship between logged values of state Medicaid recipient populations and state Medicaid program expenditures. This important substantive finding probably would have been missed if there had not been a great deal of attention paid to the details of the scatterplot in Figure 3.1B.

Enhancements for Bivariate Scatterplots

A basic scatterplot is an extremely powerful tool for visualizing bivariate data. There are several enhancements that can be added to this kind of display to provide more information about features such as the underlying pattern of the data, the univariate distributions of the constituent variables, and the individual observations in the data set.

Jittering for Overplotting and Repeated Data Points

Overplotting occurs in bivariate scatterplots for two main reasons: (a) paired continuous variables with relatively dense concentrations of data points at particular regions within their bivariate distribution and (b) discrete variables in which the number of distinct data values is relatively small compared to the range of the data and the number of observations. In both situations, jittering can be used to eliminate excessive overlap among the plotted points (e.g., Chambers et al., 1983).[18]

A. Poorly-Constructed Scatterplot

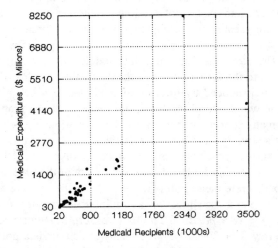

B. Better Version of the Scatterplot

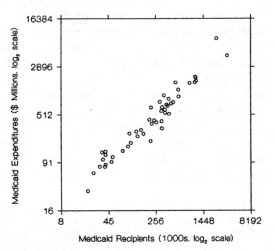

Figure 3.1. Relationship Between Medicaid Population Sizes and Medicaid Program Expenditures in the Uniated States, 1986
SOURCE: U.S. Department of Health and Human Services.

As explained in Chapter 2, jittering introduces a small amount of random noise into the data to produce slight shifts in the point positions within a graph. In a bivariate scatterplot, random numbers usually are added to the values of both variables. The objective is merely to break up exact over-plotting, not to change the general locations of the points within the data rectangle. Therefore, the magnitude of the random component must be very small relative to the actual ranges of the data values.

The effects produced by jittering discrete data can be quite dramatic. Consider the two scatterplots shown in Figure 3.2. Each graph shows the results from an experiment that examined the relationship between knowl-edge about a stimulus and affect toward that stimulus. In the experiment, 470 participants were shown a picture of a stimulus object. They then were provided with varying levels of information about the object—from zero through six discrete facts. Following that, participants were asked to rate their feelings about the object on a 7-point scale ranging from 1 = *very negative* to 7 = *very positive*. The first scatterplot (Figure 3.2A) simply graphs the raw data. Visually, there seems to be one data point plotted at each of 44 distinct locations (out of the 49 separate combinations that are possible). What really is occurring is severe overplotting; there are many separate data points, but they are laid precisely on top of each other at most of the plotting positions within the graph. Of course, this prevents accurate visual decoding of the underlying structure among these two variables.

Figure 3.2B repeats the same scatterplot with the data points jittered to break up the overplotting. Now data points that share the same values on the two variables are clustered around their respective locations rather than plotted at a single common position. The relative concentrations of points can be discerned through the areas covered by the clusters and/or the density of the ink used to draw each of the clusters. In either case, the jittered scatterplot reveals that the strongest concentration of observations falls along a generally diagonal band in the middle of the data rectangle. This shows that increasing amounts of information do tend to coincide with more positive evaluations of the stimulus object. This is a potentially important substantive observation. But the discrete nature of the data caused the relevant structure to be hidden within the original nonjittered scatterplot.

Marginal Box Plots

Sometimes it is useful to include univariate distributional information within a bivariate scatterplot. Doing so simply increases the overall amount

A. Scatterplot Using Original, Discrete Data Values

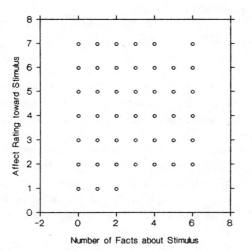

B. Scatterplot Using Jittered Data Values

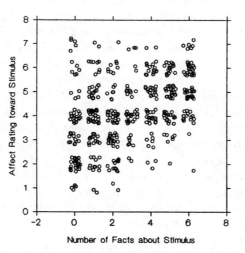

Figure 3.2. Relationship Between Information About a Stimulus Object and Affect Toward That Stimulus
SOURCE: Responses obtained from 470 experiment participants.

of information contained within the single graphical display. Supplemental displays of univariate information also provide cues that help readers take into account features such as asymmetry and outliers when they decode the information from the scatterplot.

The basic idea is very simple: Place a univariate graph into the top horizontal margin of the scatterplot to represent graphically the distribution for the X variable, and place another univariate graph into the right vertical margin, thereby supplying the same information for the Y variable. Box plots are the best type of univariate display for inclusion in a scatterplot for several reasons. They can be made very thin (the width of the box is arbitrary and does not correspond to any aspect of a variable's distribution), they can be interpreted easily in either a horizontal or vertical orientation, they provide an immediate visual representation of important distributional characteristics (particularly the medians and the quartiles as measures of center and spread in the respective distributions), and they provide a representation of the data that is visually quite distinct from that used in the scatterplot itself (i.e., boxes rather than individual data points).

Figure 3.3 shows an example of a scatterplot with marginal box plots. The graph contains data on 1991 crime rates in the United States; specifically, the rates of reported burglaries within the states are plotted against the corresponding rates of reported robberies. The shape of the point cloud indicates that these variables are moderately related to each other; as one would expect, states with high robbery rates tend to show relatively high burglary rates and vice versa. However, it also is important to note that this pattern is far from clear-cut; there are quite a few states that show high levels for one type of crime and relatively low levels for the other. Visual inspection of the box plot for state burglary rates (shown in the right vertical margin of the display) indicates that the latter are distributed symmetrically around a median of about 1,200 (the exact value for this median actually is 1,158). By contrast, the box plot for state robbery rates (shown horizontally across the top of the scatterplot) reveals a positively skewed distribution with two high outliers. This may indicate a need to transform the X variable to produce a more symmetric array of points in the horizontal direction. At a minimum, readers should take the asymmetry into account as they decode the information from the graph. In any event, the differing univariate distributions would have been much harder to detect from the basic scatterplot alone.

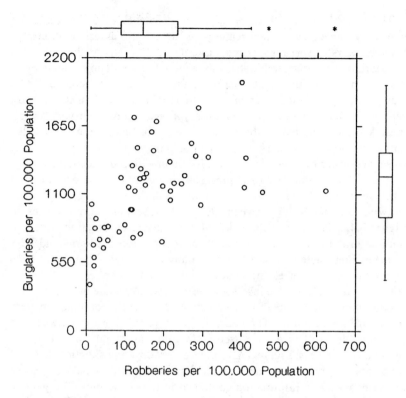

Figure 3.3. Robbery Rates Versus Burglary Rates in the United States, 1991
SOURCE: *Statistical Abstract of the United States*, 1992.

Labeling Points

Point labels can be used to identify the locations of specific observations within the scatterplot. Although this enhancement may add to the overall amount of information contained in the graphical display, it often produces results that are unsatisfactory for purposes of data visualization.[19] The problem is that space usually is tight around the plotted points within the data rectangle. Therefore, labels often overlap each other and render themselves illegible. Even worse, the labels usually overlap some of the data points, thereby degrading visual perception of the quantitative information.

These problems are alleviated somewhat by the fact that point labeling is usually unnecessary when scatterplots are used to assess relationships between pairs of variables. In that case, the emphasis is on the shape and orientation of any discernible structure within the overall point cloud rather than on the individual points that make up the cloud.[20] Of course, it still may be useful to identify *certain* points in a scatterplot such as those representing outliers and other unusual observations. But by their very nature, these kinds of data tend to be located at some distance from most of the remaining observations. Therefore, it should be relatively easy to find the space necessary to insert short labels for them within the scatterplot.

Figure 3.4 presents two examples, showing good and bad uses of point labels in scatterplots. The data are identical to those presented in Figure 3.3 showing the relationship between 1991 state robbery and burglary rates. In Figure 3.4A, labels are supplied for three unusual observations: the two outliers in the univariate distribution of robbery rates (Illinois and New York) and one state that shows an unusually high level of burglaries even though it falls close to the central region of the robbery distribution (Florida). In this case, the labels are used to identify some of the observations that exhibit the greatest discrepancies from the predominant pattern in the full set of points. The generally positive relationship between the two variables still is easily discernible from the cloud formed by the remaining 47 points. Figure 3.4B shows a very different situation. Here all 50 points are given labels, and it is much more difficult to make any sense of the quantitative information contained in the scatterplot. The general conclusions are quite simple: Avoid the "blind" use of point labels whenever possible. In situations where labels are necessary, use them selectively to highlight particularly interesting observations within the graphical display.[21]

Slicing a Scatterplot

One of the great strengths of a scatterplot is that it enables a researcher to evaluate the relationship (if any exists) between the two variables included in the graphical display. The visual nature of this assessment is very important because it avoids the a priori assumptions that provide the basis for more traditional numerical summaries of statistical relationships (such as the linearity assumption underlying the use of Pearson product-moment correlations and regression analysis). Instead, visualization facilitates the

A. Only Unusual Data Points are Labelled

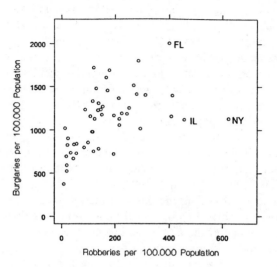

B. All Data Points are Labelled

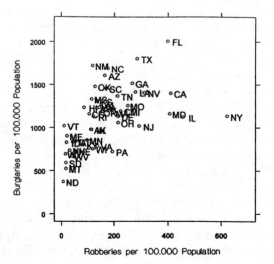

Figure 3.4. Robbery Rates Versus Burglary Rates in the United States, 1991
SOURCE: *Statistical Abstract of the United States*, 1992.

identification of relationships and underlying patterns that may not conform to any simple structure (Chambers et al., 1983).

In a scatterplot, a relationship exists when points that have different coordinates on one scale axis also tend to exhibit systematically different coordinates on the other scale axis. If two variables are related to each other, then the plotted points will not be distributed uniformly throughout the entire data rectangle. Instead, the point cloud will form some pattern or shape. However, noisy data and weak interrelationships often inhibit visual identification of any such patterns. Furthermore, even if a general pattern can be discerned in the graph, it can be difficult to characterize its precise nature through simple visual inspection of the scatterplot alone.

One way of dealing with this problem is to divide one dimension of the scatterplot (usually the horizontal) into segments (or slices) and examine the conditional distribution of the other variable within each slice (e.g., Chambers et al., 1983; Cleveland, 1993b). Variations across the Y variable's conditional distributions provide information about the relationship between the two variables. In principle, the conditional distributions could be represented by any of the univariate displays discussed in Chapter 2. However, box plots are particularly useful in this situation because they can easily be fit within the vertical slices of the X variable values, even when the latter are quite narrow.

Figure 3.5 shows an example of a sliced scatterplot. The figure contains data on 94 nations. The X variable is 1980 per capita gross national product (GNP), and the Y variable is the 1980 infant mortality rate per 100,000 population. Figure 3.5A shows a basic scatterplot of these data; note that both axes are shown with logarithmic scales (Base 10) to correct for positive skewness in the two variables. The same scatterplot is shown in the next panel (Figure 3.5B), but vertical dotted lines have been added to show how the GNP variable is sliced into five equally sized intervals. Finally, Figure 3.5C shows the box plots for the conditional distributions of infant mortality within each slice of the GNP variable.

From inspection of the conditional median lines in Figure 3.5C, it immediately is clear that these variables have a negative but curvilinear relationship. Furthermore, the residual spread around this negative trend seems to be greatest in the central region of the logged GNP distribution (the boxes are largest and the whiskers are longest for the central three box plots). Finally, there are several outliers including two nations with very large GNP values and unusually high infant mortality rates. Thus a sliced scatterplot immediately conveys a great deal of detailed information about a bivariate relationship.

63

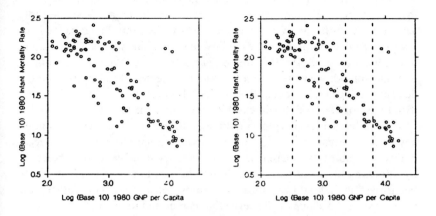

A. Basic Scatterplot

B. Slicing Intervals

C. Box Plots from Sliced Scatterplot

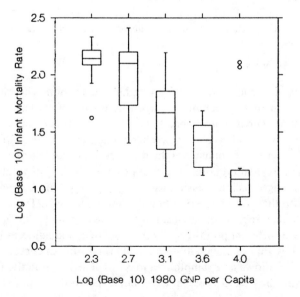

Figure 3.5. Slicing a Scatterplot of the Relationship Between 1980 GNP per Capita and Infant Mortality Rates
SOURCE: Friendly (1991).
NOTE: GNP = gross national product.

Nonparametric Scatterplot Smoothing

Another strategy for illustrating the relationship between two variables involves fitting a smooth curve to the points in the bivariate scatterplot. The purpose of the curve is to summarize how the central tendency of the Y variable's distribution changes at different locations within X's distribution (Chambers et al., 1983). If the two variables are unrelated to each other, then the smooth curve will be a flat line (the center of the Y distribution does not change regardless of the X value). If the two variables are related, then the smooth curve should exhibit some other shape.

The challenge in scatterplot smoothing is to fit a curve to the data without any detailed advance specification of the functional relationship between the two variables. Nonparametric smoothers try to achieve this objective by following the empirical concentration of the plotted points. The resultant fitted "line" should pass through the most dense areas of the data region regardless of the shape of the curve that is required to do so.

There are a number of nonparametric smoothers available (Goodall, 1990), including those based on running medians (Hartwig & Dearing, 1979; Tukey, 1977; Velleman & Hoaglin, 1981), kernel estimators (Härdle, 1991; Hastie & Tibshirani, 1990), splines (Eubank, 1988; Shikin & Plis, 1995), and the loess smoother (Cleveland & Devlin, 1988; Cleveland, Devlin, & Grosse, 1988). Of these, the latter probably is the most popular and commonly used. Therefore, it is the only one that is discussed here.

The Loess Smoother

Loess is an acronym for *lo*cally weighted regre*ss*ion. The method is a generalization of the technique known as lowess, for *lo*cally *w*eighted *s*catterplot *s*moother (Cleveland, 1979). The loess procedure is computationally intensive and involves a number of distinct steps. Essentially, loess performs a series of robust weighted regressions at each of m different locations or evaluation points (v_j, with j running from 1 to m) along the X variable's range; each regression uses only the subset of observations that fall close to that evaluation point on the horizontal axis. The coefficients from each local regression are used to generate a predicted or fitted value, $g(v_j)$. The m different points (v_j, $g[v_j]$) are plotted, and adjacent points are connected by line segments to produce the final smooth curve.

Figure 3.6 shows an example of a loess fit. The graph in the first panel of the figure shows 1992 per capita welfare expenditures within the United

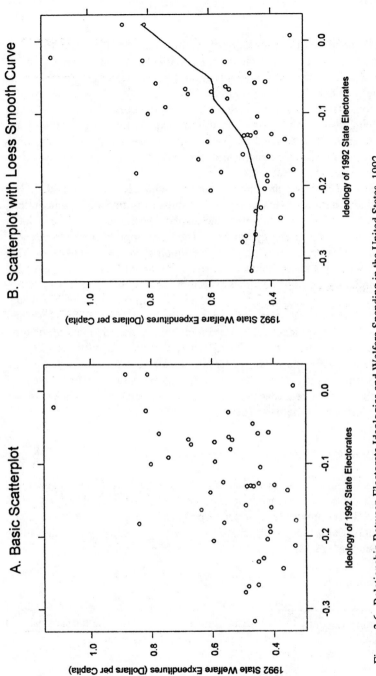

A. Basic Scatterplot

B. Scatterplot with Loess Smooth Curve

Figure 3.6. Relationship Between Electorate Ideologies and Welfare Spending in the United States, 1992

SOURCE: Welfare spending data obtained from the *1992 Statistical Abstract of the United States* and the state electorate ideologies provided by Gerald C. Wright.

States plotted against a measure of the ideologies of the respective state electorates. The latter variable is coded so that larger values correspond to states whose citizens are relatively more likely to describe themselves as "liberal" rather than "conservative" and vice versa for smaller values (Erikson, Wright, & McIver, 1993). The diagonal orientation of the point cloud suggests that ideology and welfare expenditures are positively related to each other. Beyond that very general observation, it is difficult to state any more specific conclusions about the relationship from the information in this basic scatterplot.

Figure 3.6B shows the same scatterplot with a loess curve added. The curvilinear nature of this positive relationship is revealed immediately. Looking from left to right within the display, the curve is relatively flat at low values of the ideology variable. Then the slope becomes noticeably steeper beginning approximately at the ideology score of –.20 or so. This is followed by a short "plateau" in the curve toward the right side of the plot, and then the slope becomes even more sharply positive. The curvilinear shape of this loess curve is important in substantive terms. As one would expect, more liberal states—those near the right side of the horizontal axis—show higher levels of welfare spending. At the other end of the plot, there appears to be a "floor effect," where welfare expenditures level off. Apparently, even the most conservative states cannot eliminate welfare expenditures entirely, so they tend to exhibit similarly low levels of spending in this area; this in turn produces the relatively shallow portion on the left side of the loess curve.

The Details of Fitting a Loess Smooth Curve

To show how the loess smoother works, Figure 3.7 provides an example using hypothetical bivariate data on 20 observations.[22] The first panel (Figure 3.7A) shows the basic scatterplot. To keep the presentation simple, the data form a fairly clear curved pattern. The steps of the loess fitting procedure are as follows.

1. Preliminaries

First, define m equally spaced locations across the range of X values. Call these v_j, where the subscript j ranges from 1 to m. The loess curve will be evaluated at each of the v_j's. The loess fitted value (i.e., the vertical coordinate for the curve) at v_j is shown as $g(v_j)$.

E. Bisquare Robust Weights.

F. Final Robust Line and Fitted Value.

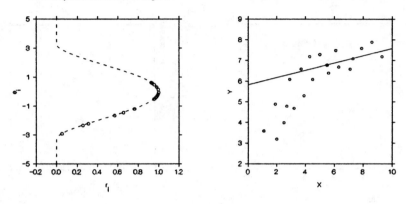

G. Complete Set of Fitted Values.

H. Loess Curve

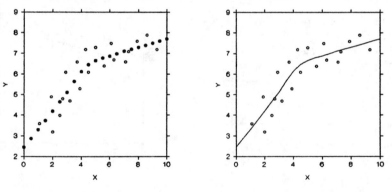

Figure 3.7. Illustration of Loess Fitting Procedure Using Hypothetical Data

Second, supply values for two parameters, α and λ. α is a value between 0 and 1 that gives the proportion of observations that are used in each of the local regressions. The number of observations used in each local regression (called "the window") then is defined as $q = \alpha n$, where n is the number of empirical data points; q is truncated to an integer, if necessary.

A. Hypothetical Data for Loess Fit.

B. Window for v_j=5.5 and α=0.6.

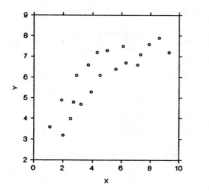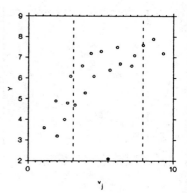

C. Tricube Neighborhood Weights.

D. Initial Regression Line and Fitted Values

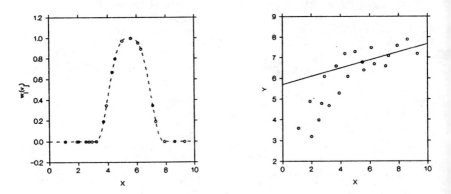

Figure 3.7. Continued

The value of λ is either 1 or 2; it gives the degree of the polynomial equation to be fitted to the data.

For the example data, there are 21 v_j values (i.e., $m = 21$) uniformly spaced in the closed interval from 0.0 to 10.0; hence $v_1 = 0.0$, $v_2 = 0.5$, and so on up to $v_{21} = 10.0$. The locations of the various v_j's are shown as tick marks on the horizontal scale of Figure 3.7B.[23] In this case, α is set to .60, and so $\alpha n = 12$. Thus the window always will enclose the 12 empirical data points that fall closest to the current v_j on the horizontal axis. Figure 3.7B shows the window for $v_j = 5.5$ (an arbitrarily selected value located by the asterisk along the horizontal axis in the figure). Note that the physical width of this window will change at different v_j's as the distance to the 12th closest data point changes. Also, evaluation points close to either the maximum or minimum values will have asymmetric windows. For example, v_1 will have all 12 points in its window arrayed to the right, whereas v_{21} will have all 12 points arrayed to its left. In any event, the window always will contain the 12 closest empirical data points regardless of their direction and/or distance from v_j.

2. For Each v_j, Calculate Neighborhood Weights

Let $\Delta_{[i]}(v_j) = |x_i - v_j|$s, the distance from the point of evaluation (v_j) to the ith observation, x_i. The brackets around the subscript indicate that these distances are sorted from smallest to largest. Then, $\Delta_{[i]}(v_j)^* = \Delta_{[i]}(v_j) / \Delta_{[q]}(v_j)$ is the same distance, expressed as a proportion of the distance from v_j to the farthest data point within the window. Thus $\Delta_{[i]}(v_j)^* \leq 1.0$ if x_i falls within the current window, and $\Delta_{[i]}(v_j)^* > 1.0$ if x_i falls outside the window.

The neighborhood weight for observation i is defined using the tricube weight function as follows:

$$w_i(v_j) = \begin{cases} [1 - |\Delta_{[i]}(v_j)^{*3}|]^3 & for\ \Delta_{[i]}(v_j)^* < 1 \\ 0 & Otherwise \end{cases} \tag{3.1}$$

Neighborhood weights are calculated for all observations, from $i = 1$ to n. The shape of the tricube weight function and the specific weights assigned to the 20 observations are shown in Figure 3.7C. Note how the observations with X values close to 5.5 have large weights near 1.0. The weights fall off fairly quickly for observations with X values substantially different (in either direction) from the current evaluation point of $v_j = 5.5$.

3. For Each v_j, Find the Fitted Value, $g(v_j)$

First, find the coefficients, b_k, that minimize the following:

$$\sum_{i=1}^{n} w_i(v_j)\ (y_i - [(\sum_{k=0}^{\lambda} b_{kj} x_i^k)])^2 \tag{3.2}$$

Because the value of λ was set to 1, a linear equation is fit to the weighted data, and Equation 3.2 can be expressed as

$$\sum_{i=1}^{n} w_i(v_j)\,(y_i - b_{0j} - b_{1j}\,x_i)^2 \tag{3.3}$$

The coefficients of the preceding equation are found using weighted least squares. The fitted value is obtained by taking the predicted value of Y at v_j:

$$g(v_j) = \sum_{k=0}^{\lambda} b_{kj}\,v_j^k \tag{3.4}$$

Once again, the linear fitting equation can be simplified to

$$g(v_j) = b_{0j} + b_{1j}v_j \tag{3.5}$$

Figure 3.7D shows the line fitted at $v_j = 5.5$, along with the point $(v_j, g[v_j])$, which is plotted as the solid circle superimposed over the line. Note how the slope of the fitted line is positive but relatively shallow. This reflects the orientation and shape of the point cloud in that region of the scatterplot. Evaluation points at different locations within the data rectangle would produce different results. For example, if v_j were closer to the left side of the plot (say, at 2.0), then the slope of the fitted line would be positive but much steeper.

4. Optional Robustness Step for Each v_j

In most loess smooths, the initial local regression line and fitted value are replaced by another line and fitted value that are obtained using a robust estimation procedure. To do this, first obtain the residuals from the preceding local regression for all n observations. For observation i,

$$e_i = y_i - \sum_{k=0}^{\lambda} b_{kj}\,v_j^k \tag{3.6}$$

Then, define e_i^* as follows:

$$e_i^* = \frac{e_i}{6\,Median\,|e_i|} \tag{3.7}$$

Use the bisquare weight function to define the robustness weight for each observation, as follows:

$$r_i = \begin{cases} (1 - |(e_i *)^2|)^2 & for \ |e_i *| < 1 \\ 0 & Otherwise \end{cases} \tag{3.8}$$

The shape of the bisquare weight function and the robustness weights assigned to the 20 observations both are shown in Figure 3.7E. Use the robustness weights to estimate a new set of coefficients, b_k*, which minimize the following expression:

$$\sum_{i=1}^{n} r_i \, w_i(v_j) \, ([y_i - (\sum_{k=0}^{\lambda} b_{kj}^* x_i^k)])^2 \tag{3.9}$$

Use the newly estimated b_k* values to obtain a new fitted value, $g(v_j)$:

$$g(v_j) = \sum_{k=0}^{\lambda} b_{kj}^* v_j^k \tag{3.10}$$

Repeat the robustness steps until the values of the estimated coefficients (or the fitted values) converge. This usually occurs very quickly, after one or two iterations. Figure 3.7F shows the robust line and final fitted value for $v_j = 5.5$. In this case, the robust fitted line is very similar to the original line because there are no serious outliers or unusual data points within the scatterplot. If there were, then the initial and final fitted lines could differ quite substantially. Therefore, this robustness step almost always is incorporated into the calculation of a loess smooth curve.

5. Repeat Steps 2, 3, and (optionally) 4 for All m Values of v_j

Figure 3.7G shows the points $(v_j, g[v_j])$ obtained by carrying out the preceding steps for all of the $m = 21$ evaluation points. The plot shows the actual data points as open circles and the loess fitted points as solid circles.

6. Draw the Fitted Loess Smooth Curve

Use line segments to connect the adjacent $(v_j, g[v_j])$ points (as shown in Figure 3.7H for the example data) and eliminate the points themselves. The latter are superfluous because they really are just a function of the arbitrarily chosen evaluation points rather than the actual data values.

Note how the final fitted curve in Figure 3.7H passes through the center of the entire point cloud as one moves from left to right through the data rectangle of the graph. In so doing, the loess curve neatly reflects the nonlinear relationship between X and Y. The remarkable thing about this smooth curve is that the loess procedure *found the shape of the plot on its own*; the evident curvilinearity did not appear as the result of any structural specification made in advance by the analyst.

Fitting Parameters and Diagnostics for the Loess Smooth Curve

Selecting the values for the loess fitting parameters is a subjective process. At the same time, analysts must use their own judgment about the adequacy with which a loess smooth curve represents the structure within the given data set. Still, the considerations that are involved in these decisions are relatively straightforward.

Specifying α, the Smoothing Parameter

In a loess fit, α gives the proportion of observations that are to be used in each local regression; accordingly, this parameter usually is specified as a number between 0 and 1. The value of α selected for any loess smooth curve has an immediate effect on the fitted curve. Larger values of α always produce smoother curves, whereas smaller values result in curves with more fluctuations, jaggedness, and "bumps." This occurs because small α values correspond to a narrow window width; only a small subset of the data are given nonzero neighborhood weights in each local regression. Therefore, the fitted line, $\sum_{k=0}^{\lambda} b_{kj}^{*} v_{j}^{k}$, and the corresponding fitted value, $g(v_{j})$, will be heavily influenced by the variability that occurs among the data values within that relatively narrow subset of observations. If there is any noise in the data (as there usually will be), then the local fits can fluctuate wildly, producing loess curves that are not very smooth. Larger α values bring more observations into each local regression. The noise variability cancels out to a greater extent within each local fit, and so the local fitted lines and values exhibit less fluctuation across the various windows (i.e., the m different v_{j} values) within the data. This in turn produces a smoother loess curve.

Figure 3.8 shows the effect of the α parameter using the data on state ideology and welfare spending. The four panels show loess curves to the same data. All of them employ λ values of 1 (locally linear fitting), but the α values are varied from .25 in the first panel up to 1.00 in the last. Clearly, the curve becomes smoother as this parameter increases. Informally, one could think of the loess curve as a string that is laid across the range of the X values within the data. The α value controls the "slackness" of this string, with larger values pulling it tighter and therefore producing a straighter curve. For this reason, α sometimes is called the "tension" parameter in the loess fit.

It is important to select the best α value for a given data set. If α is too large, then the loess fit will produce an overly smoothed curve, which may miss important features of the data; Cleveland (1993b) calls this situation "lack of fit." For example, the loess fit in Figure 3.8D is extremely smooth, with very little curvature. However, it fails to pass through the center of the point cloud. Most of the data points in the central region of X values (between about $X = -.25$ and $X = -.05$) fall below the loess curve. Therefore, the latter does not provide an accurate representation of the original data.

On the other hand, a very small α value can produce a curve that follows the data too closely—a situation that Cleveland (1993b) calls an "excess of fit." Superficially, this may not seem to be a problem; after all, the objective is to generate a model that conforms as closely as possible to the empirical data that it is intended to represent. However, some of the empirical variation within any data set consists of "noise" that is not substantively interesting. When α is too small, the resultant loess curve will track this noise variation closely. In so doing, it becomes more difficult to discern any structural variability that may exist within the data points. This situation is represented by the jagged loess curve shown in Figure 3.8A. Here the gyrations of the fitted curve do not appear to provide any useful insights regarding the functional relationship between the two variables; instead, the curve simply follows "clumps" of data points within the overall point cloud.

The most appropriate α value for any given scatterplot is determined through an analysis of the loess residuals. The general objective is to produce a loess curve that is as smooth as possible but still captures all of the relevant structure existing within the data. The loess residuals measure the variability in the Y variable that remains after the dispersion of the fitted values (and hence the smooth curve) is taken into account. To the extent that the loess curve does summarize the important features of the bivariate data, there should be no discernible pattern within the residuals. Any systematic interdependencies between X and Y should be picked up in the loess fitting process itself.

A. Loess Curve with α = 0.25

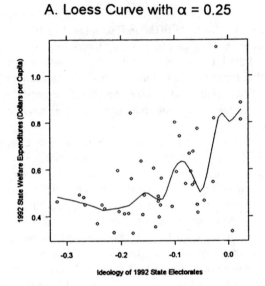

B. Loess Curve with α = 0.50

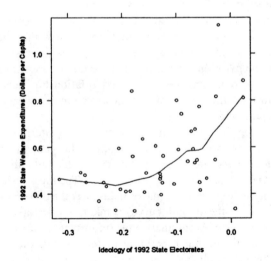

C. Loess Curve with α = 0.80

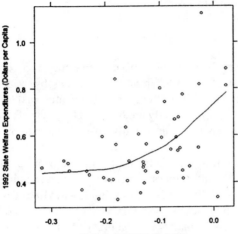

D. Loess Curve with α = 1.00

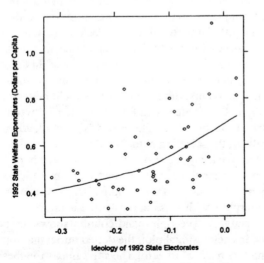

Figure 3.8. Effect of the α Parameter on the Loess Smooth Curve
SOURCE: Welfare spending data obtained from the *1992 Statistical Abstract of the United States* and the state electorate ideologies provided by Gerald C. Wright.

The loess residuals are defined as the difference between the observed values of the Y variable and the corresponding fitted values for the respective occurrences of the X variable values:

$$e_i = y_i - g(x_i) \qquad (3.11)$$

Note that the m evaluation points used to find the loess curve (v_j with $j = 1, 2, \ldots m$) usually are different from the n observed values of the independent variable, X. Therefore, the fitted values on the right-hand side of Equation 3.11, $g(x_i)$, typically are obtained by interpolating between the two closest occurrences of the equally spaced evaluation points (i.e., the v_j's).

As a diagnostic test, the e_i's from Equation 3.11 are plotted against the original X variable and a loess curve is fitted to the points. The smooth curve in this residual plot should approximate a flat line. This indicates that there is no further structure in the data that were "missed" by the initial loess fit. If the loess fit in the residual plot does show some nonhorizontal pattern, then the original loess analysis needs to be repeated with different values substituted for the fitting parameters.[24]

The strategy for selecting the proper smoothing parameter value is to start with a relatively small α (say, .25 or so). Check the residual plot for this initial smooth curve; it almost always will indicate an adequate fit to the data. But some of this fit will involve the noise in the data, which should be eliminated from the smooth curve. Therefore, repeat the loess fit to X and Y using a slightly larger α value and check the residual plot (including its own loess curve) for nonhorizontal patterns that would signal the presence of "leftover" structure in the data. Repeat this process until the residual plots begin to indicate that the smooth curve is missing important features in the data points; the final α value should be the one just before this occurs. Typically, α values will fall somewhere between about .40 and .80, although there are many exceptions to this generalization. In any actual empirical analysis, the selection of the α value always will have to be made through the iterative trial-and-error process described here.

Figure 3.9 illustrates the use of residual plots in the loess fit using the data on state ideology and welfare spending. In the left column, the panels show the scatterplots with loess curves fitted using α values of .25, .50, and 1.00, respectively. The right-hand column shows the corresponding residual plots. In each residual plot, the dotted horizontal line is a baseline corresponding to a residual of zero. The solid line is the loess curve fitted to the observed residuals. When $\alpha = .25$, the fitted line in the residual plot is very flat, showing that there is no structure remaining in the residuals. However, the loess fit for the original data is not very smooth, indicating that the curve probably incorporates a great deal of noise variation. At the other extreme, the loess fit based on $\alpha = 1.00$ inadequately represents an important feature of the data—the curvilinear nature of the relationship between ideology and welfare spending. This is indicated by the "depression" in the residual plot, showing that there is additional structure remaining in the data after the loess curve is fit to X and Y.

The middle row of Figure 3.9 shows a compromise between the two extreme situations. The loess curve is fit to the data using $\alpha = .50$. This produces a fairly smooth, easily described curve without an excess of fit. Also, inspection of the residual plot reveals that the smooth curve fitted to the residuals is flat. This shows that the loess fit to state electorate ideology and state welfare spending captures all of the discernible structure in the data points. For these reasons, it is the loess curve obtained using $\alpha = .50$ that would be reported and subjected to closer examination.

Specifying λ, the Degree of the Loess Polynomial

The λ parameter determines the degree of the polynomial fit in each local regression. When $\lambda = 1$, linear equations are fit within each of the windows on the data. When $\lambda = 2$, a quadratic equation is used. The choice between these two specifications is relatively straightforward. If the point cloud in the scatterplot conforms to a generally monotonic pattern, then $\lambda = 1$ should be specified. In this case, the m different local fitting windows all will contain subsets of points with similar general orientations (i.e., the local point clouds will show either monotonically increasing or monotonically decreasing patterns). Linear regression lines always should produce reasonable summaries of these local point clouds, even though their specific slopes and intercepts may differ markedly across the respective evaluation points, v_j.

If the data exhibit some nonmonotone pattern with local minima and/or maxima, then specifying $\lambda = 2$ for quadratic local regressions produces a better fit. In this case, the orientation of the point cloud will change across the local fitting windows; some subsets of the data points will exhibit monotonically increasing patterns, whereas other subsets contain point clouds that tend to spread in the opposite direction (i.e., monotonically decreasing orientation). The predominant pattern within the data set changes direction, and such reversals cannot be handled very effectively with linear equations. The quadratic specification allows for inflections

A1. Loess Curve Fitted with α = 0.25

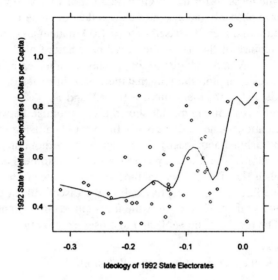

A2. Residual Plot for α = 0.25 Loess Fit

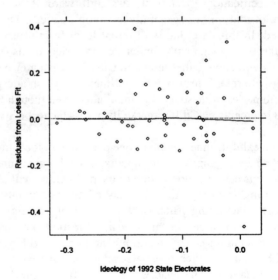

B1. Loess Curve Fitted with α = 0.50

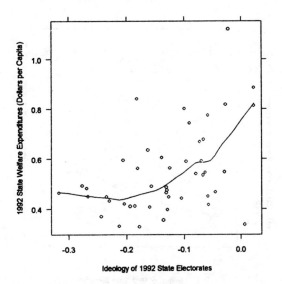

B2. Residual Plot for α = 0.50 Loess Fit

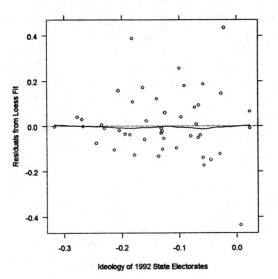

Figure 3.9. Smooth Curves and Residual Plots Obtained for Loess Fits to Data on 1992 State Ideologies and Welfare Spending

C1. Loess Curve Fitted with α = 1.00

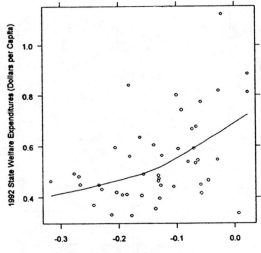

C2. Residual Plot for α = 1.00 Loess Fit

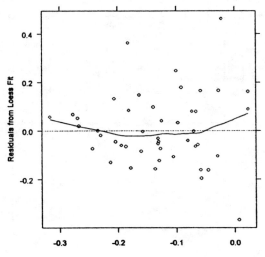

(continued)

within the fitted curve that can be used to deal with local minima and maxima. Thus locally quadratic equations introduce the flexibility that is required to fit a loess curve that tracks accurately through the center of a nonmonotone point cloud.

Figure 3.10 demonstrates how locally quadratic fitting can produce a more accurate loess smooth curve in certain situations. The figure shows data on self-identified Democrats' preferences between Walter Mondale and Gary Hart over the course of the 1984 presidential primary campaign. The first panel contains a loess curve with $\lambda = 1$. Even though the smoothing parameter is set to a reasonable value ($\alpha = .50$), the curve fails to track the data points accurately in the "peaks" and "valleys" that occur in the scatterplot. Specifically, note that the fitted line has a negative slope near the left side of the plot. However, most of the data points at the extreme left fall below the line; the latter clearly does not pass through the center of the point cloud in this region of the data. Another serious problem exists in the region from about 50 to 100 on the horizontal axis. Here the curve does not dip low enough to follow accurately the sizable set of data points that occur in that region of the scatterplot.

The second panel in Figure 3.10 shows the same scatterplot. However, the loess curve now has been fitted with $\lambda = 2$ (α remains at .50). With this modification, the fitted curve tends to pass through the center of the point cloud at all locations throughout the set of plotted points. Exactly as expected, the most pronounced changes occur in the regions at the extreme left and in the center of the plot. The smooth curve in this display suggests that Mondale's support peaked and then fell off during the early days of the 1984 campaign. This differs markedly from the locally linear fit, which seemed to indicate that Mondale simply began the campaign with steadily declining support. The locally quadratic fit also shows that the decline in Mondale's support was very sharp during the middle of the campaign period; this feature is much more pronounced than it was in the loess fit based on locally linear equations. Thus the effects of the λ specification are serious enough that they influence the substantive interpretations drawn from the scatterplot. For now, however, the important conclusion is that the locally quadratic fitting procedure tends to follow the rather extreme undulations in the plotted data. This in turn ensures that the loess smooth curve provides a relatively accurate representation of the original data points.

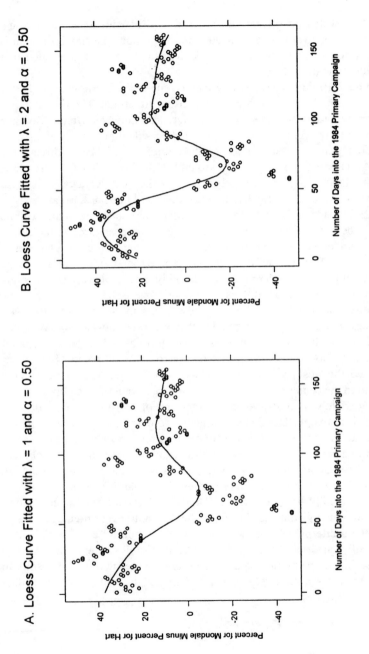

Figure 3.10. Public Preferences Between Walter Mondale and Gary Hart (among Democrats only) During the 1984 Presidential Primary Campaign

SOURCE: 1984 Continuous Monitoring Survey, with data modified by the author.

Goodness of Fit for a Loess Smooth Curve

When a smooth curve is fitted to a scatterplot, attention usually is focused on the shape of the curve because this is most revealing of the structure within the data. However, it still is important to consider goodness of fit, that is, how well the smooth curve characterizes the empirical data values. A useful graphical display for doing so is the *R-F* (residual-fit) *spread plot* (Cleveland, 1993b). This display consists of the empirical quantile plot for the loess fitted values (the $g[x_i]$ values), placed alongside the empirical quantile plot for the loess residuals (the e_i values, as defined in Equation 3.11). Both of these variables are centered so as to express them as deviations about their respective means; however, their values still are measured in the units of the original Y variable, and so the two distributions can be compared to each other directly. Ideally, the fitted values should be arrayed across a wider range than the residuals, indicating that the loess smooth curve accounts for most of the variance in the dependent variable.

Figure 3.11 shows two examples of R-F spread plots. Note that grid lines are included in each display to facilitate comparisons of the monotone point arrays across the panels. Figure 3.11A shows the R-F spread plot for the loess smooth curve of the state welfare spending data. At first glance, the spread of the residuals is much greater than the spread of the fitted values. However, there are several prominent large residuals—one strong negative outlier in the lower left corner of the residual spread plot and two or three positive outliers in the upper right-hand corner. Once these unusual observations are removed from consideration, the amount of spread is very similar across the fitted values and the residuals. From this evidence, it appears that the unexplained variability in state welfare spending is about equal to that accounted for by the loess smooth curve.

Figure 3.11B shows the R-F spread plot for the loess fit to the Mondale-Hart preference data. Again, a quick glance might suggest that there is roughly equal spread in the fitted values and the residuals. However, as we already saw in the original scatterplot, there are some outliers and these are affecting the R-F spread plot. The lowest four residuals and the highest three residuals all are unusually large; they definitely "stand apart" from the remainder of the quantiles in the plot. If we ignore these outliers, then the spread of the fitted values clearly is greater than the spread of the remaining nonoutlying residuals. This in turn suggests that Mondale-Hart preferences did vary markedly over time during the 1984 presidential campaign.

84

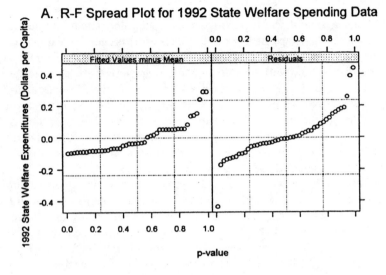

A. R-F Spread Plot for 1992 State Welfare Spending Data

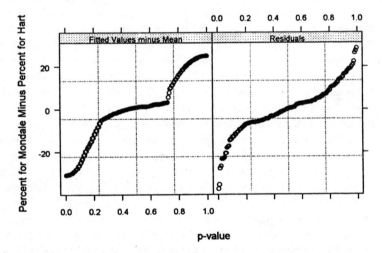

B. R-F Spread Plot for 1984 Democratic Candidate Preference

Figure 3.11. Two Examples of R-F Spread Plots for Loess Smooth Curves

Aspect Ratio and Banking to 45 Degrees

When a smooth curve is fitted to a set of plotted points, it is particularly important that the researcher be attentive to the aspect ratio of the graphical display (Cleveland, 1993b, 1994). This is defined as the physical height of the data rectangle divided by the width. Any smooth curve is actually composed of a number of smaller straight-line segments, which are joined at their end points. Human perception of the smooth curve is affected by differences in the orientations of the constituent line segments. The sizes of these differences are themselves determined by the aspect ratio of the scatterplot.

With too large an aspect ratio, the vertical scale of the graph will be greatly spread out relative to the horizontal scale of the graph. The line segments that constitute any smooth curve in that graph will be "stretched" in a vertical direction, and it will be extremely difficult to discern accurately the differences in their exact orientations. Too small an aspect ratio has a similar effect, with the line segments stretched in a horizontal direction. Thus the accuracy of the visual decoding process is strongly influenced by the aspect ratio of a scatterplot containing a smooth curve.

Visual perception of smooth curves should be most accurate when the differences in the slopes of the line segments making up that curve are as large as possible. Theory and experimentation both indicate that this objective is achieved when the mean absolute orientation of the line segments is set to 45 degrees, or a mean slope of 1.0 (Cleveland, 1993b; Cleveland, McGill, & McGill, 1988). This provides an objective for graph construction: Cleveland recommends that the aspect ratio (and hence the physical shape) of any scatterplot containing a smooth curve should be set so that the mean absolute orientation of the constituent line segments is 45 degrees. The process used to achieve this orientation is called *banking to 45 degrees*.

The process of banking is straightforward, but it is rather tedious in computational terms. Therefore, readers are referred to Cleveland (1993b, 1994) for the details. But the effect of banking on the accuracy of graphical perception can be demonstrated quite easily and dramatically. Figure 3.12 shows some hypothetical smoothed data on monthly voter registration figures, plotted over a 10-year period. The first panel (Figure 3.12A) uses an aspect ratio of 1.0. From the curve, we can see what appears to be a 4-year cycle with a large spike in presidential election years, a slump in the nonelection year, a smaller spike for the off-year elections, and another nonelection year slump.

A. Aspect Ratio Set to 1.0

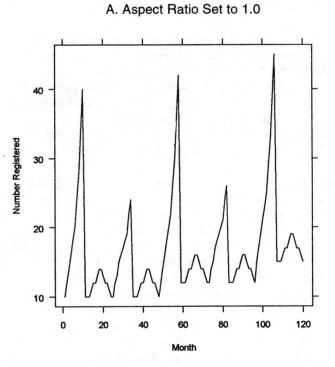

B. Aspect Ratio Banked to 45 Degrees

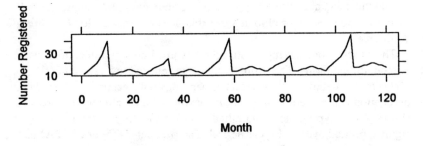

Figure 3.12. Plot of Hypothetical Data on Voter Registration Figures, by Month, to Show the Effects of Aspect Ratio on Visual Perception
SOURCE: Data created by the author.

Figure 3.12A actually hides an interesting detail in the data because the aspect ratio of the graphical display is too large. New information is revealed in Figure 3.12B, in which the aspect ratio has been banked to 45 degrees. Here it is clear that the drop-off in registrations following a spike is much sharper than the gradual increase in registration numbers that occurs on the "leading edge" of each spike.

The only thing that changes across the two graphs in Figure 3.12 is the aspect ratio. But this has a strong effect on the information that is drawn from the display. Clearly, Figure 3.12B shows more detail in the data than does Figure 3.12A. Thus banking definitely is a worthwhile addition to a smoothed scatterplot. Cleveland recommends that banking to 45 degrees be applied routinely to graphical displays containing smooth curves to maximize the effectiveness of the visual decoding process.

Conclusions

This chapter has shown how two-dimensional scatterplots can provide useful graphical summaries of the structure in bivariate data. In terms of Cleveland's visual perception model, the scatterplot construction guidelines and enhancements described in this chapter should facilitate detection of the data points. Procedures such as slicing and nonparametric smoothing encourage the visual assembly that is necessary to evaluate functional dependencies. Finally, banking to 45 degrees should encourage accurate visual estimation of both the data values and the relationships between variables.

Graphical presentations of bivariate data often are more revealing than numerical summaries. Descriptive statistics, such as correlation coefficients, measure only the degree to which the data conform to a particular kind of structure (usually linear). By contrast, a scatterplot shows all of the data rather than some abbreviated summary. Therefore, visual processing of the graphical information allows the researcher to discern many kinds of patterns, internal structures, and features that would be completely hidden in the value of a single descriptive statistic. Thus graphical displays of bivariate data can be used to obtain important insights without strong a priori assumptions about the exact nature of any relationship that may exist between two variables.

4. CONCLUSIONS

This monograph has presented some basic tools for statistical graphics. Specifically, the discussion has covered methods for displaying univariate and bivariate data along with some general ideas and principles that are applicable to virtually any pictorial display of quantitative information. In closing this discussion, there are three important points that deserve further emphasis.

First, statistical graphics involves more than merely drawing pictures of data. Instead, it comprises an ongoing process of graphing and fitting (Cleveland, 1993b). *Graphing* techniques provide analysts with techniques for examining information to discern any coherent structure that may exist therein. *Fitting* procedures supply the means for imposing mathematical functions onto the data to characterize that structure as succinctly as possible. This process almost always is iterative in nature. A graph provides clues about the appropriate type of function for the data at hand. Then the resultant fit suggests further graphical views of the data (the residuals from the fit, transformations of the original data values, etc.), which lead to further fitting, and so on. The ultimate objective of this process is exactly the same as that of traditional statistics and data analysis: a parsimonious model or abstraction that provides useful insights about the phenomenon under investigation. The graphical approach to data analysis really only differs from traditional methodology in the precise steps that are taken to achieve this objective.

Second, graphical methods try to provide a *look* at the data without presupposing the nature of the view that will result. In other words, the visualization techniques covered in this monograph try to impose minimal assumptions about the nature of any structure in the data. Even the simplest traditional statistical methods (e.g., linear regression models) are based on very stringent assumptions about the nature of the processes generating the observed data (e.g., Berry, 1993). Once such assumptions are made, the researcher is more or less committed to a particular analytical direction. Therefore, he or she is less likely to pursue, or even notice, departures from the assumptions that may occur in the data. The standard (although frequently misleading) reassurance is that most statistical techniques are relatively robust against violations of their underlying assumptions. Although this may be true, it is not really the point. Rather than *force* an inaccurate model onto uncooperative data, it is more productive to *look* directly at the data and use any resultant insights to specify a model that does provide an accurate representation of the empirical information. Statistical graphics provide many tools that are useful for this purpose.

Third, and finally, the material covered in this monograph is important in its own right, but it also represents just the beginning of a much broader subject area. The discussion so far has been limited to fairly simple research situations involving variables taken singly or two at a time. But this is not likely to be sufficient for at least two reasons. On the one hand, social and political phenomena are inherently complex; most interesting variables have multiple sources and/or consequences. On the other hand, most social scientific research is nonexperimental in nature; the effects of extraneous variables cannot be subsumed within a randomization process like that which undergirds experimental designs. For these reasons, multivariate analyses and models almost always are necessary; additional sources of variability in data typically are handled by introducing additional dimensions into a quantitative model (e.g., Jacoby, 1991). But this creates new challenges for statistical graphics because visual depictions almost always are represented on two-dimensional surfaces such as a piece of paper or a computer screen. Fortunately, there are a variety of graphical display strategies that are applicable to multivariate data; in fact, many of them are extensions of the techniques discussed in the earlier chapters of this monograph. They will be taken up within the companion volume in this series, *Statistical Graphics for Visualizing Multivariate Data*.

NOTES

1. Several writers have used this strategy to illustrate the advantages obtained by inspecting graphical displays of quantitative information. They include Anscombe (1973), Cleveland (1985, 1994), Fox (1991), Friendly (1991), and Tufte (1983).

2. Strictly speaking, this discussion covers only one part of Cleveland's graphical perception theory, called *pattern perception*. Along with this component, he also identifies another conceptually distinct aspect of visual processing, called *table look-up*. The latter involves using elements of a graphical display to obtain scale information about the data values; for example, visually scanning from the top of a specific bar in a bar chart over to the vertical axis and then reading off the tick values from the scale to determine the approximate number or percentage of observations that fall within a particular category. In view of the earlier discussion about tabular versus graphical displays, I would argue that table look-up is less important (at least for present purposes) than pattern perception. If the analyst needs to know precise quantitative information, then he or she can simply identify the data point in question and retrieve the specific value from a table of the original data. This is a particularly easy process given the massive information retrieval capabilities of modern computing equipment.

3. All of the graphs in this volume were created on a personal computer with a 133-megahertz Pentium processor. The graphs were constructed using the Trellis Graphics System in S-Plus for Windows, Version 3.3 (Becker & Cleveland, 1995; Becker, Cleveland, Shyu, & Kaluzny, 1995) and Systat for Windows, Version 5 (Wilkinson, Hill, Micelli, Birkenbeuel, & Vang, 1992).

4. There are no general clear-cut criteria for selecting appropriate bin sizes for histograms. However, guidelines and rules of thumb are provided in a number of different sources including Doane (1976), Emerson & Hoaglin (1983), Scott (1979), and Terrell and Scott (1985).

5. One way of overcoming this problem is to use a stem-and-leaf display (Emerson & Hoaglin, 1983; Tukey, 1977), which is similar to a histogram but shows actual data values within the bins. This kind of display is covered in the Quantitative Applications in the Social Sciences (QASS) volume by Hartwig and Dearing (1979), and a more recent discussion is provided in Fox (1990).

6. Most treatments of smoothed histograms take a statistical perspective and assume that the purpose of the display is to estimate an underlying population density. The present discussion takes a more data analytic perspective and merely assumes that the smoothed histogram is intended to provide a useful summary of the information contained in a set of univariate data.

7. The total area under the density trace usually is somewhat less than 1.0, for reasons explained in Note 10. Although perhaps inelegant in mathematical terms, this is not problematic for visual assessments of the distribution. As explained in Chapter 1, exact numerical values are not recovered very accurately from graphical displays, and the slight departures from a total area of 1.0 will have little effect on visual estimates of proportionate areas under the curve.

8. In a histogram with bar heights adjusted by $1/2h$ factor (i.e., the total area under the histogram bars is 1.0), the contribution of each observation also would be $1/n$. In that case, a single observation's contribution could be visualized as a rectangle, spread evenly across the entire width of the bin into which the observation falls.

9. The m different evaluation points, v_j, usually begin and end at the extremes of the empirical data, that is, $v_1 = x_{min}$ and $v_m = x_{max}$. In this hypothetical example, v_1 has been set to 0 and v_m to 9.5, even though these values extend beyond the range of the data. This is done merely for the sake of simplicity in the example.

10. Note that the density trace seems to end abruptly at the horizontal positions corresponding to the minimum and maximum evaluation points, v_1 and v_{20}. It does not drop down to the origin on the vertical axis either at or beyond these locations. In any real use of a smoothed histogram, these extreme evaluation points would be located at the minimum and maximum observed data values. Therefore, anchoring the density trace at these positions prevents the smoothed histogram from extending beyond the actual range of the observed data. This is also the feature that causes the total area under the density trace to be less than 1.0. Again, this does not cause any problems for interpretation of the graphical display.

11. There also are adaptive kernel density estimators (Silverman, 1986) that adjust the bandwidth according to the local density of the data. Specifically, the bandwidth is made narrower in areas of the variable's range that contain many data points; the band is widened in sparse segments of the data distribution.

12. Like the sizes of the bins in a histogram, the bandwidth in a smoothed histogram is arbitrary. If one is willing to make assumptions about the shape of the underlying probability density (usually, that it is Gaussian or normal), then there are criteria for selecting the bandwidth that attempt to minimize the variance and the bias in the empirical estimate of the density (e.g., Härdle, 1991; Silverman, 1986). Of course, one of the main reasons for using a smoothed histogram is precisely that we are unwilling to make such assumptions; therefore, these criteria are only of limited utility for exploring univariate data. Furthermore, these guidelines can produce particularly misleading results when the true underlying distribution is quite different from the one that is assumed (e.g., when a distribution that is assumed to be Gaussian is in reality multimodal). For these reasons, it probably is safest to use a trial-and-error approach in determining the bandwidth to be used for any particular data set. One strategy would be to start with a relatively small value of h (relative to the range of the data) and inspect the resultant smoothed histogram. Then, gradually increase the h value and examine the impact on the smoothed histogram, stopping when the degree of smoothness seems to hide features that were prominent in the shape of the distribution at lower h values.

13. Because the vertical axis of a univariate scatterplot is not substantively interpretable or important, it usually is not shown in the display.

14. Empirical observations usually do not fall at specific "important" quantiles such as the median. Therefore, it often is necessary to interpolate between the nearest empirical quantiles. Interpolation is very simple (Chambers et al., 1983; Cleveland, 1994): The p value of the desired but unobserved p^{th} quantile (X_p) falls some fraction, f, of the distance from the two closest observed p values, which are denoted $p*$ and $(p* + 1)$. Then

$$X_p = (1 - f)X_{p*} + fX_{p*+1}$$

For example, assume that we want to obtain the 0.25 quantile from the data in Table 2.1. There is no observation with a p value of exactly 0.25. However, there are observed $X_{0.245}$ and $X_{0.265}$; these quantiles correspond to data values 176 and 177, respectively. The desired p value (0.25) falls $f = 0.25$ of the distance from 0.245 to 0.265. Plugging these values into the preceding interpolation formula yields

$$Xp = (0.75)176 + (0.25)177 = 176.25$$

Thus the 0.25 quantile for this distribution, $X_p = 176.25$.

15. There are many variants of box plots. For discussions and some examples, see McGill, Tukey, and Larsen (1978) and Tufte (1983).

16. Other useful discussions about the issues involved in constructing scatterplots can be found in Friendly (1991), Kosslyn (1994), Tufte (1983), and Tukey (1977). Note, however, that all of these authors frequently disagree with each other in their guidelines and recommendations.

17. Unfortunately, space considerations preclude a thorough treatment of transformations in this monograph. Nevertheless, it is a topic that is of vital importance for the effective graphical display of data. Relevant sources include Emerson (1983), Emerson and Stoto (1983), Hines and Hines (1987), Stoto and Emerson (1984), and Tukey (1977). In the QASS series, the monograph by Fox (1991) contains an excellent summary discussion of data transformations.

18. A sunflower plot is another strategy for dealing with overplotting (Cleveland & McGill, 1984b). In this kind of display, the number of observations that occur at a single position is encoded into the plotting symbol used at that position. Specifically, a single observation is shown as an open circle, and additional data points are represented as radial line segments emanating from the circle. When several observations occur together, the resultant plotting symbol resembles a flower with the radial lines as the petals—hence the name *sunflower plot*.

19. It is surprisingly difficult to devise a general procedure that places point labels into a scatterplot and still provides an accurate visual representation of the data. See Kuhfeld (1986) and Noma (1987) for two different strategies aimed at dealing with this problem.

20. Labels are much more important when the information in the scatterplot is interpreted as a data map (e.g., Greenacre, 1984). This commonly occurs in the output from scaling procedures such as factor analysis, multidimensional scaling, and correspondence analysis (e.g., Jacoby, 1991). In maps, attention usually is focused on relationships between the plotted points (such as interpoint distances or angles), and so the specific identities of the objects being plotted are important for interpreting the graphical display. Fortunately, the number of points in a data map usually is relatively small, so labeling is not problematic.

21. Scatterplot brushing (Becker & Cleveland, 1988) is an alternative strategy that is useful in some situations. This involves moving a pointing device (such as a mouse cursor) across a scatterplot shown on a computer display to cause changes in the points that are touched by the pointer. In this context, the label would appear for brushed points.

22. This discussion draws heavily from the excellent presentation in Cleveland (1993b).

23. In any real application of loess, the v_j's would only range across the observed values of the X variable. For this example, the evaluation points are evenly spaced across the interval from 0 to 10 to keep the v_j's at simple round values.

24. It also is useful to examine the scatterplot of the absolute values of the loess residuals against the X variable, or against the fitted values ($g[x_i]$), to see whether the spread of the Y values is functionally related to X (e.g., Chambers et al., 1983; Cleveland, 1993b). This display often is called a *spread-location (S-L) plot* (Emerson & Strenio, 1983). Once again, a loess curve can be fitted to the points in the S-L plot. If the smooth curve is flat, then it indicates homoscedastic residuals from the loess smooth fit to the original data. A nonflat loess curve in the S-L plot would be evidence that Y's dispersion is affected by the X variable.

REFERENCES

ANSCOMBE, F. J. (1973) "Graphs in statistical analysis." *American Statistician* 27: 17-22.

BECKER, R. A., CHAMBERS, J. M., and WILKS, A. R. (1988) *The New S Language: A Programming Environment for Data Analysis and Graphics.* Pacific Grove, CA: Wadsworth and Brooks/Cole.

BECKER, R. A., and CLEVELAND, W. S. (1988) "Brushing scatterplots." In W. S. Cleveland and M. E. McGill (eds.), *Dynamic Graphics for Statistics.* Belmont, CA: Wadsworth and Brooks/Cole.

BECKER, R. A., and CLEVELAND, W. S. (1995) *S-Plus Trellis Graphics User's Manual, Version 3.3.* Seattle, WA: Mathsoft, Inc.

BECKER, R. A., CLEVELAND, W. S., SHYU, M., and KALUZNY, S. (1995) "A tour of Trellis Graphics." Unpublished manuscript. (Available on World Wide Web at http://netlib.att.com/netlib/att/stat/info/trellis.html)

BENIGER, J. R., and ROBYN, D. L. (1978) "Quantitative graphics in statistics: A brief history." *The American Statistician* 32: 1-11.

BERRY, W. D. (1993) *Understanding Regression Assumptions* (Sage University Paper series on Quantitative Applications in the Social Sciences, series no. 07-092). Newbury Park, CA: Sage.

BERTIN, J. (1981) *Graphics and Graphic Information-Processing.* New York: Walter de Gruyter.

BERTIN, J. (1983) *Semiology of Graphs.* Madison: University of Wisconsin Press.

CHAMBERS, J. M., CLEVELAND, W. S., KLEINER, B., and TUKEY, P. A. (1983) *Graphical Methods for Data Analysis.* Pacific Grove, CA: Wadsworth and Brooks/Cole.

CLEVELAND, W. S. (1979) "Robust locally weighted regression and smoothing scatterplots." *Journal of the American Statistical Association* 74: 829-836.

CLEVELAND, W. S. (1984) "Graphical methods for data presentation: Full scale breaks, dot charts, and multibased logging." *The American Statistician* 38: 270-280.

CLEVELAND, W. S. (1985) *The Elements of Graphing Data.* Pacific Grove, CA: Wadsworth and Brooks/Cole.

CLEVELAND, W. S. (1993a) "A model for studying display methods of statistical graphics." *Journal of Computational and Graphical Statistics* 2: 323-343.

CLEVELAND, W. S. (1993b) *Visualizing Data.* Summit, NJ: Hobart.

CLEVELAND, W. S. (1994) *The Elements of Graphing Data* (rev. ed.). Summit, NJ: Hobart.

CLEVELAND, W. S., and DEVLIN, S. J. (1988) "Locally weighted regression: An approach to regression analysis by local fitting." *Journal of the American Statistical Association* 83: 596-610.

CLEVELAND, W. S., DEVLIN, S. J., and GROSSE, E. (1988) "Regression by local fitting: Methods, properties, and computational algorithms." *Journal of Econometrics* 37: 87-114.

CLEVELAND, W. S., and McGILL, M. E. (1988) *Dynamic Graphics for Statistics*. Pacific Grove, CA: Wadsworth and Brooks/Cole.

CLEVELAND, W. S., McGILL, M. E., and McGILL, R. (1988) "The shape parameter of a two-variable graph." *Journal of the American Statistical Association* 83: 289-300.

CLEVELAND, W. S., and McGILL, R. (1984a) "Graphical perception: Theory, experimentation, and application to the development of graphical methods." *Journal of the American Statistical Association* 79: 531-553.

CLEVELAND, W. S., and McGILL, R. (1984b) "The many faces of a scatterplot." *Journal of the American Statistical Association* 79: 807-822.

CLEVELAND, W. S., and McGILL, R. (1985) "Graphical perception and graphical methods for analyzing and presenting scientific data." *Science* 229: 828-833.

CLEVELAND, W. S., and McGILL, R. (1987) "Graphical perception: The visual decoding of quantitative information on graphical displays of data." *Journal of the Royal Statistical Society* 150: 192-229.

COOK, R. D., and WEISBERG, S. (1994) *An Introduction to Regression Graphics*. New York: John Wiley.

DOANE, D. P. (1976) "Aesthetic frequency classifications." *The American Statistician* 30: 181-183.

EHRENBERG, A. S. C. (1975) *Data Reduction*. New York: John Wiley.

EMERSON, J. D. (1983) "Mathematical aspects of transformation." In D. C. Hoaglin, F. Mosteller, and J. W. Tukey (eds.), *Understanding Robust and Exploratory Data Analysis* (pp. 247-282). New York: John Wiley.

EMERSON, J. D., and HOAGLIN, D. C. (1983) "Stem-and-leaf displays." In D. C. Hoaglin, F. Mosteller, and J. W. Tukey (eds.), *Understanding Robust and Exploratory Data Analysis* (pp. 7-32). New York: John Wiley.

EMERSON, J. D., and STOTO, M. A. (1983) "Transforming data." In D. C. Hoaglin, F. Mosteller, and J. W. Tukey (eds.), *Understanding Robust and Exploratory Data Analysis* (pp. 97-128). New York: John Wiley.

EMERSON, J. D., and STRENIO, J. (1983) "Boxplots and batch comparison." In D. C. Hoaglin, F. Mosteller, and J. W. Tukey (eds.), *Understanding Robust and Exploratory Data Analysis* (pp. 58-94). New York: John Wiley.

ERDMAN, K., and WOLFE, S. M. (1987) *Poor Health Care for Poor Americans: A Ranking of State Medicaid Programs*. Washington, DC: Public Citizen Health Research Group.

ERIKSON, R. S., WRIGHT, G. C., and McIVER, J. P. (1993) *Statehouse Democracy: Public Opinion and Public Policy in the American States*. Cambridge, England: Cambridge University Press.

EUBANK, R. L. (1988) *Spline Smoothing and Nonparametric Regression*. New York: Marcel Dekker.

FOX, J. (1990) "Describing univariate distributions." In J. Fox and J. S. Long (eds.), *Modern Methods of Data Analysis*. Newbury Park, CA: Sage.

FOX, J. (1991) *Regression Diagnostics*. Newbury Park, CA: Sage.

FOX, J. (1992) "Statistical graphics." In E. F. Borgatta and M. L. Borgatta (eds.), *Encyclopedia of Sociology*. New York: Macmillan.

FRIENDLY, M. (1991) *SAS System for Statistical Graphics, First Edition*. Cary, NC: SAS Institute, Inc.

GNANADESIKAN, R. (1977) *Methods for Statistical Analysis of Multivariate Data*. New York: John Wiley.

96

GOODALL, C. (1990) "A survey of smoothing techniques." In J. Fox and J. S. Long (eds.), *Modern Methods of Data Analysis.* Newbury Park, CA: Sage.

GREENACRE, M. J. (1984) *Theory and Applications of Correspondence Analysis.* London: Academic Press.

HÄRDLE, W. (1991) *Smoothing Techniques With Implementation in S.* New York: Springer-Verlag.

HARTWIG, F., and DEARING, B. E. (1979) *Exploratory Data Analysis.* Beverly Hills, CA: Sage.

HASTIE, T. J., and TIBSHIRANI, R. J. (1990) *Generalized Additive Models.* New York: Chapman & Hall.

HENRY, G. T. (1995) *Graphing Data: Techniques for Display and Analysis.* Thousand Oaks, CA: Sage.

HINES, W. G. S., and HINES, R. J. O. (1987) "Quick graphical power-law transformations selection." *The American Statistician* 41: 21-24.

HOAGLIN, D. C. (1985) "Using Quantiles to Study Shape." In D. C. Hoaglin, F. Mosteller, and J. W. Tukey (eds.), *Exploring Data Tables, Trends, and Shapes.* New York: John Wiley.

JACOBY, W. G. (1991) *Data Theory and Dimensional Analysis.* Newbury Park, CA: Sage.

KOSSLYN, S. M. (1985) "Graphics and human information processing: A review of five books." *Journal of the American Statistical Association* 80: 499-512.

KOSSLYN, S. M. (1989) "Understanding charts and graphs." *Applied Cognitive Psychology* 3: 185-225.

KOSSLYN, S. M. (1994) *Elements of Graph Design.* New York: Freeman.

KUHFELD, W. F. (1986) "Metric and nonmetric plotting models." *Psychometrika* 51: 155-161.

McGILL, R., TUKEY, J. W., and LARSEN, W. A. (1978) "Variations of box plots." *The American Statistician* 32: 12-16.

MILLER, G. A. (1956) "The magic number seven, plus or minus two." *Psychological Review* 63: 81-97.

MOSTELLER, F., and TUKEY, J. W. (1977) *Data Analysis and Regression.* Reading, MA: Addison-Wesley.

NOMA, E. (1987) "A heuristic method for label placement in scatterplots." *Psychometrika* 52: 463-468.

SCOTT, D. W. (1979) "Optimal and data-based histograms." *Biometrika* 66, 605-610.

SHIKIN, E. V., and PLIS, A. I. (1995) *Handbook on Splines for the User.* Boca Raton, FL: CRC.

SILVERMAN, B. W. (1986) *Density Estimation for Statistics and Data Analysis.* New York: Chapman & Hall.

SIMKIN, D., and HASTIE, R. (1987) "An information-processing analysis of graph perception." *Journal of the American Statistical Association* 82: 454-465.

SPENCE, I. (1990) "Visual psychophysics of simple graphical elements." *Journal of Experimental Psychology: Human Perception and Performance* 16: 683-692.

SPENCE, I., and LEWANDOWSKY, S. (1990) "Graphical perception." In J. Fox and J. S. Long (eds.), *Modern Methods of Data Analysis.* Newbury Park, CA: Sage.

STINE, R., and FOX, J. (eds.) (1996) *Statistical Computing Environments for Social Research.* Thousand Oaks, CA: Sage.

STOTO, M. A., and EMERSON, J. D. (1984) "Power transformations for data analysis." In Samuel Leinhardt (ed.), *Sociological Methodology, 1983-1984*. San Francisco: Jossey-Bass.

TARTER, M. E., and KRONMAL, R. A. (1976) "An introduction to the implementation and theory of nonparametric density estimation." *The American Statistician* 30: 105-112.

TERRELL, G. R., and SCOTT, D. (1985) "Oversmoothed nonparametric density estimates." *Journal of the American Statistical Association* 80: 209-214.

TIERNEY, L. (1990) *Lisp-Stat: An Object-Oriented Environment for Statistical Computing and Dynamic Graphics*. New York: John Wiley.

TUFTE, E. R. (1983) *The Visual Display of Quantitative Information*. Cheshire, CT: Graphics Press.

TUFTE, E. R. (1990) *Envisioning Information*. Cheshire, CT: Graphics Press.

TUKEY, J. W. (1977) *Exploratory Data Analysis*. Reading, MA: Addison-Wesley.

VELLEMAN, P. F., and HOAGLIN, D. C. (1981) *Applications, Basics, and Computing of Exploratory Data Analysis*. Boston: Duxbury.

WILK, M. B., and GNANADESIKAN, R. (1968) "Probability plotting methods for the analysis of data." *Biometrika* 55: 1-17.

WILKINSON, L., HILL, M., MICELLI, S., BIRKENBEUEL, G., and VANG, E. (1992) *Systat for Windows: Graphics, Version 5 Edition*. Evanston, IL: Systat, Inc.

YOUNG, F. W. (1996) *ViSta: The Visual Statistics System*. Chapel Hill, NC: L. L. Thurstone Psychometrics Laboratory.

YOUNG, F. W., FALDOWSKI, R. A., and HARRIS, D. F. (1990) "The spreadplot: A graphical spreadsheet with algebraically linked plots." In *Proceedings: American Statistical Association, Section on Statistical Graphics*, pp. 42-47.

YOUNG, F. W., FALDOWSKI, R. A., and McFARLANE, M. M. (1993) "Multivariate statistical visualization." In C. R. Rao (ed.), *Handbook of Statistics* (Vol. 9). New York: Elsevier.

ABOUT THE AUTHOR

WILLIAM G. JACOBY is Associate Professor in the Department of Government and International Studies at the University of South Carolina. He received his B.A. from the University of Delaware and his M.A. and Ph.D. in Political Science from the University of North Carolina at Chapel Hill. Along with statistical graphics, his major areas of interest include measurement and scaling methods, public opinion, and political behavior. Dr. Jacoby is the author of *Data Theory and Dimensional Analysis* (Sage, 1991) and has published articles in journals such as the *American Journal of Political Science*, *The Journal of Politics*, and *Political Analysis*.

Quantitative Applications in the Social Sciences

A SAGE UNIVERSITY PAPER SERIES

$10.95 each

To order, please use order form on the next page.

107063

Quantitative Applications
in the Social Sciences

A SAGE UNIVERSITY PAPER SERIES

$10.95 each

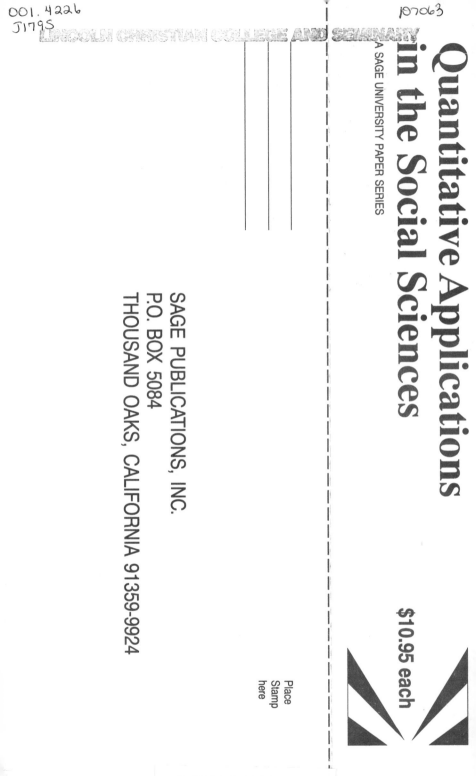

SAGE PUBLICATIONS, INC.
P.O. BOX 5084
THOUSAND OAKS, CALIFORNIA 91359-9924

Place
Stamp
here